The Wines of Long Island

The Wines of Long Island
Birth of a Region

Philip F. Palmedo and Edward J. Beltrami

Photographs by
Sara Matthews

With a Preface by Paul Pontallier,
General Manager, Château Margaux

Waterline Books
Great Falls, Virginia

This is a **Waterline** Natural History Book

WATERLINE BOOKS
438 River Bend Road
Great Falls, VA 22066
(703) 759-2440

ISBN: 0-9628492-1-9

Design and Composition: Greta D. Sibley

Cover: Renee Chituk, at the Jamesport Country Kitchen,
  with a sampling of Long Island Wines

First Printing, 1993

Contents

ACKNOWLEDGEMENTS vii

PREFACE ix

CHAPTER 1

Introduction: Creation & Discovery 1

CHAPTER 2

Soil, Grapes & Wine 7

The Long Island Terroir • The Grapes Of Long Island • The Whites: *Chardonnay, Sauvignon Blanc, Gewürztraminer, Riesling, Pinot Blanc, Chenin Blanc* • The Reds: *Merlot, Cabernet Sauvignon, Pinot Noir, Cabernet Franc* • Other Wines • From Grapes To Wine

CHAPTER 3

The Historical Legacy 31

The Early Days • Long Island's Early Wines • The East End • Legislation • Word Gets Around • The Selling Of The Wines • *Recent Long Island Vintages: 1985-1992*

CHAPTER 4

Vineyards & Wineries 49

Hargrave Vineyard • Bridgehampton Winery • Pindar Vineyard • Lenz Winery • Bedell Cellars • Palmer Vineyards • Gristina Vineyards • Bidwell Vineyards • Le Rève/Southhampton • Paumanok Vineyards • Jamesport Winery • Mattituck Hills Winery • Peconic Bay Vineyards • Pellegrini Vineyards • Pugliese Vineyards • Banfi Vineyards at Old Brookville

CHAPTER 5

Supporting Cast 123

North Fork Wine Services • Cornell Cooperative Extension Service Of Long Island • Ressler Vineyards • John Ross • *Ross' Summer Lobster Stew*

CHAPTER 6

Conclusion: Imaginary Balloons, Reputation & Romance 133

Style • Quality • Reputation • Romance

MAP 138

NOTE TO THE FIRST TIME VISITOR 140

BIBLIOGRAPHY 142

INDEX 144

ABOUT THE AUTHORS 149

Acknowledgments

This book took some time to find its appropriate balance and tone, and the advice of several friends was helpful in that process. Jerome Smith was an early and knowledgeable collaborator on the book, and his voice can still be heard in its pages. We benefited from the advice, both linguistic and cultural, of Peter White and Chris Palmedo. The enthusiasm of the experienced publisher, Eleanor Rawson, was encouragement when we most needed it.

Our wives, Betsy Palmedo and Barbara Beltrami, were ever supportive and cheerfully imaginative in creating multiple course dinners to place tastings of Long Island and related wines in their appropriate context.

We could not have been more fortunate in our publishers. Charles Nichols and Kyrill Schabert of Waterline Books combine a feeling for Long Island with a skilled sensitivity to the language that made our work together a pleasure.

Most importantly, we would like to drink a toast to Long Island's winery owners and talented winemakers who were unfailingly generous with their time, their knowledge and their wines, even when they had more important things to do in their vineyards and cellars. They turned what could have been a difficult chore into a delightful experience. They have created an important new wine region and have given fresh life to a beautiful corner of the earth. We dedicate this book to them.

Preface

I was first introduced to winemaking on Long Island when I had the pleasure of participating in the Symposium on Maritime Climate Winegrowing that was held on the beautiful East End in July, 1988. I was struck by several things during the days I spent on Long Island that summer: the strong connections with our winemaking traditions in Bordeaux, the kindness and the adventurous spirit of the winemakers and vineyard owners and the remarkable quality of the wines.

We are very proud of the centuries-old traditions that we carry forward as we make wines in France. The qualities of our wines derive from those traditions and the superb endowments of soil and weather with which we are blessed. But those inheritances — and the laws that control our winemaking practices — are also constraints on our freedom. I must confess that I was somewhat envious of the freedom with which Long Island winemakers could approach the creation of an entirely new wine region. At the same time, I was impressed by the knowledge and respect that Long Islands winemakers had concerning winemaking practices and traditions in other parts of the world, particularly Bordeaux.

I detected on Long Island a strong sense of community — both from a local perspective, and with the broader wine-making community of the world. My visit there was brief, but I felt I made friends among these knowledgeable, enthusiastic, hospitable, warm Long Island winemakers.

And I was impressed, very impressed by the quality of the wines that I tasted on Long Island, particularly some beautiful Merlots and Chardonnays. On the French time scale, Long Island is in its infancy as a wine region, and it will be years, if not decades before its full potential is realized. But its promise is formidable.

I am delighted that those qualities of the new Long Island wine region that struck me at the time of my first visit: the kindness and adventurous spirit of the people, the reflections of winemaking traditions in France, the beauty of the region and the high quality of the wines have now been so well captured by Philip Palmedo's and Edward Beltrami's text and through Sara Matthews' sensitive photographs. I only wish that the early, formative days in the history of Bordeaux had been captured with the care, intelligence and affection that come through so clearly in this fine volume.

Paul Pontallier
General Manager, Château Margaux
March 5, 1993

Winter/Spring. *Repositioning pruned canes, Palmer Vineyards.*

CHAPTER I

Introduction: Creation & Discovery

"Long Island…there, Colonel Gibbs, from whose garden the Isabella came, amused himself with a vineyard, as did Colonel Spooner; there, poor Loubat struggled and failed to compel vinifera to grow on a commercial scale; and there the learned Prince poured out, through his catalogues and monographs, information to the country at large…"

—Thomas Pinney
A History of Wine in America
from the Beginnings to Prohibition

Creation is an apt term to describe the activities of the wine pioneers, investors, grape growers and winemakers who have turned the East End of Long Island into the most exciting new wine region in the country. However, discovery is also an apt term. Michelangelo described his sculpture as the release of forms latent in the marble he carved. Many of Long Island's winemakers feel the same way. They are convinced that the region has very special endowments of climate and soil, and that noble wines are, in a sense, latent there, waiting to be discovered.

Alex and Louisa Hargrave were the first of the modern viticultural pioneers to suspect the latent potential in the soils of eastern Long Island. The original spark struck on Thanksgiving, 1972, when they stopped by the Wickham Fruit Farm in Cutchogue on the North Fork. They had been searching on both coasts for a favorable place to grow grapes and to make wine. When they saw the fresh vegetables brought in from the nearby fields on that mild November day, they knew they had found, in Louisa's words, "a little garden of Eden."

Like many great discoveries, the logic of the Hargrave's decision seems obvious in retrospect. They recognized that the waters of Long Island Sound and the Atlantic produce a climate on the East End of Long Island that is remarkably similar to the climate some 5,000 miles to the East, on the shores of Bordeaux. The well-drained, sandy loam soils also seemed ideal. They planted their first grapes on seventeen acres in Cutchogue in the spring of 1973 and sold their first wines four years later. The grape varieties they chose to plant were those that produce the great wines of the world: Cabernet Sauvignon, Merlot, Pinot Noir, Chardonnay and Riesling.

Although the Hargraves were the first to commercialize wines from eastern Long Island, they were not the first to try. That honor may belong to a certain Moses "The Frenchman" Fournier, who, legend has it, grew wine grapes in Cutchogue in the 1680s. Although it is speculated that Mr. Fournier grew European grape varieties, it is highly unlikely that he grew them successfully.

There were numerous attempts in the seventeenth and eighteenth centuries to grow European grapes in this country, some of them major efforts. They all failed, however, because of the vines' susceptibility to various diseases and pests that were unknown in their native lands. By the early 1800s these problems had been solved, and several European wine grape varieties were successfully grown in Flushing, not far from New York City. At the time the Hargraves discovered the East End, a European variety of table grape was being grown by John Wickham in Cutchogue.

In the late 1970s, word of interesting wines started to percolate back from the East End. The Hargraves were written up in the *New Yorker* and *The New York Times*. Soon other pioneer winemakers followed in their footsteps. The next wineries to be established were Pindar Vineyards, The Lenz Winery and Bridgehampton Winery, the latter being the first to stake a claim to the South Fork.

By the mid-1980s, Long Island wines started to catch the attention of wine experts. Even in its early years, Leon D. Adams recognized the potential of the region, and in his authoritative *Wines of America*, published in 1985, he proclaimed that "the still largely rural eastern half of Long Island [could be] the future Pauillac and Côte d'Or of New York." *The Wine Spectator* declared on its November, 1988 cover that, "Long Island has arrived," and the New York wine public, perhaps the most sophisticated in the world, gradually came to realize that a major wine region was at their doorstep. Never before had a wine region and its reputation grown as fast.

The men and women who are the principal players in this story are an extraordinarily diverse group of people: a computer engineer, who learned how to make wine in Kuwait; a local contractor; a fifth generation Long Island farmer; the granddaughter of one time Socialist Presidential Candidate, Norman Thomas; the grandson of Konstantin Frank, who proved that European grapes could grow in the Eastern United States; and young winemakers who learned their craft in Germany, France, California, Hawaii, Portugal and Australia. They are now competing with each other to make and sell the finest wines, but their common concerns and visions, and the common traditions on which they draw, are creating a legitimate culture not unlike those of the major, traditional wine growing regions of the world.

The French region of Bordeaux, with its grand châteaux imperiously set above ageless vineyards, may epitomize the romantic notion of wine culture, but the wines of the more humble and agriculturally oriented Burgundy need pay homage to no one. Burgundy's important towns wear modest clothes, however. Gevrey Chambertin, for example, is reached by following a narrow vineyard road just to the West of National Route 74, a few miles south of Dijon. A battered sign whispers, as though from a previous century, that you are approaching Gevrey Chambertin, population 1,850. If it weren't for that hallowed name, one would take this for just another of the innumerable archaic farming villages that dot every region of France. Rising to the West, however, are the slopes that produce one of the most sublime wines in the world. Chambertin was the favorite wine of Napoleon, whose armies lugged cases of it on his campaign in Egypt and to the disastrous winter in Russia. The greatness of French wines is rooted in such humble villages throughout France.

Similarly, Cutchogue, the center of Long Island's fledgling wine industry, does not have the appearance of being the capital of much of anything, except, perhaps, normalcy. One stop light designates the main intersection, where a few stores cluster. There is a drug store, a bank and a clean, white, Presbyterian church. Sidewalks extend only one block on either side of the intersection, then give way to lawns and fields that directly border the main road. It is the home of over half of the East End vineyards, and its reputation as the hub of eastern United States winemaking is growing rapidly.

The wine industry has a major significance for Long Island's East End. That part of the Island, particularly the land stretching out to the northeast of Riverhead, the North Fork, is a traditional agricultural area. And, typical of such areas in the eastern United States, it has been threatened by the seemingly inevitable encroachment of housing developments and strip malls. To the East End farmer, the financial rewards of growing cauliflower and potatoes have, at best, remained static over the years, while the offers of the developers continually escalate. Growing grapes and making wine is one of the few agricultural activities that can compete economically with conventional development— if the wine is good enough.

*   *   *

Pioneer winemakers of Long Island have now discovered the potential for fine wine which lay buried in the soils of the East End for so long, and they are well on their way to realizing that potential. But this book is also about discovery in another sense: the pleasures derived by wine lovers in discovering new wines and an entirely new wine region. We provide information to facilitate the reader's own discovery of the region's vineyards and wines. This process can always be carried out in restaurants or with the help of your local wine shop, but the most enjoyable and instructive path is found by visiting the vineyards themselves, and meeting the people who are tending the vines and making the wine. The region is worth a detour, as they say in the Michelin Guide.

All of the wineries welcome visitors. Despite their growing fame, these are mostly family enterprises, and the visitor is welcomed with a friendly hospitality. One often meets the owner or winemaker, particularly if the vineyard is visited during the week. Most wineries depend on sales from their tasting rooms for a significant fraction of their income. There are often special bottlings that can only be bought at the winery; a late harvest wine produced in very small quantities, for example. Some wineries provide informative tours. They often host special events such as concerts or barbecues, always accompanied by their wines, of course.

We should say something about how we describe and evaluate wines. Both describing wines and evaluating them are no simple matters, as the human vocabulary is very weak in matters of taste and smell. Although there have been attempts to develop a consistent vocabulary of wine tastes, those systems ultimately depend on analogies and comparisons. Wines are termed "thin," "lively" or "round," for example, or they are said to have the flavor of raspberries or to be peppery. We will use such terms, and attempt to describe what we mean by them, but we recognize that there are no absolutes in matters of taste.

We have avoided the common practice of rating wines, giving them marks between fifty and one hundred like so many math quizzes. In describing the wines of Long Island we use straight-forward terms, guided by the belief that wine quality is a multi-dimensional affair. Mostly, wine is drunk before or with a meal and the real question is, "What is appropriate," not, "What has the highest rating on a scale of one to one hundred." A Beef Wellington, candlelight dinner deserves quite a different wine than an al fresco picnic lunch by the shore. Long Island produces wines suitable for both occasions, and almost any other you can imagine. Individual taste, the nature of the occasion, the season, the company and one's budget all play a part in deciding what is appropriate.

It is an unfortunate fact of Long Island wine life that the outstanding wines of a given vintage are sold out quite quickly. Thus, rather than trying to evaluate specific wines of a specific vintages, we have attempted to describe the character of each vineyard's wines and to indicate which vineyards are apt to produce the best examples of various varieties. Many of the vineyards on Long Island have been established for sufficiently long that they have a consistent, characteristic style.

There have been very few defective wines made on Long Island in recent years. The experience of Long Island wine makers and the current technology of winemaking have all but ruled out bad wines. The few we have come across simply have not been mentioned. Price is always a factor, and we point out some wines as good buys.

Summer. *Old and new vines, Pellegrini Vineyards.*

    We have used small gatherings of wine enthusiasts to compare groups of similar Long Island wines, and to compare them with wines from the same grapes produced elsewhere in the world. These tastings have also served to broaden the opinions reflected in this book. Nevertheless, we do not believe that wine experts should presume to judge for everyone or for every occasion. We hope that our descriptions of wines and vineyards will entice you to become your own expert on Long Island wines, for the full story is only hinted at in this book. Fortunately, it is still out there to be told by the grape growers, the farmers, the vintners, the restaurateurs and, particularly, by the wines themselves.

Fall. *Merlot grapes into the hopper, prior to pressing, Pindar Vineyards.*

CHAPTER 2

Soil, Grapes & Wine

*"Wines express their source with exquisite definition.
They allow us to eavesdrop on the murmurings of the Earth."*
—Matt Kramer
Making Sense of Wine

What is it that produces a great wine? This question has perplexed wine makers and consumers for thousands of years, and it remains the subject of hot debate. On the surface, the question has a simple answer. Producing a fine wine requires the correct combination of three factors: the physical environment, the grape varieties used, and the techniques of vine management and wine making. Reaching consensus on the correct combination of these factors, of course, is the trick to the riddle. There is no magic formula for a great wine, but thousands of years of experimentation and discovery have provided some guidance for the modern winemaker.

The Long Island Terroir

Nature's role in creating a fine wine is captured in part by the notion of terroir. There is no term in English that is equivalent to the French *terroir,* nor as richly evocative. The word encompasses all of the elements of soil, landscape and climate at a specific location. These elements determine the quality of the grapes grown there and, ultimately, the quality of the wines made from them. In France, terroir is usually used to describe the characteristics of a particular wine growing commune, a specific property within the commune, or even a small parcel of land (a *cru* in Burgundy.) The emphasis in the French usage is on the chemical and physical properties of the land, and the micro-organisms of the soil (terroir also means soil or earth in French). But the concept also includes the tilt and exposure of the land, the distribution of rainfall and sun over the year and all of the other vagaries of microclimate. For example, is the soil porous or does it retain moisture? Is it rich in calcium, iron and other minerals? Is the site less prone to hail or heavy rain than another property? Does it have an advantageous southern exposure?

These and other questions identify the factors that are viewed as significant in giving one wine-producing zone, or an estate within that zone, an edge in making great wines. What is more, terroir is the major factor in determining a wine's personality: the characteristics that distinguish it from wines made elsewhere, even when the same grape types are used. Wines made from Pinot Noir grapes cultivated in Chambertin are unmistakenly different from those made from the same variety in Oregon or the Rheinfalz. Not necessarily better, but clearly different.

It is also undeniable that differences in aroma and flavor may exist between wines vinified in an identical manner from the same grape clones in two parcels only a few meters apart. Those differences in nuance are persistent and characteristic. They spell the difference, for example, between the wines from the vineyards of Perrières and Charmes in Meursault, or between those of Monprivato and Villero in Castiglione Falleto. In Bordeaux, such fine distinctions of terroir are often blurred by the tendency of Chateaux winemakers to blend vats from grapes grown in different vineyard plots.

What defines Long Island's terroir? The characteristic that is most obvious is its climate: the sunniest in New York State, with temperatures moderated by the surrounding waters. This climate is quite similar to that of the Médoc in Bordeaux and also not very different from that of Burgundy. Indeed, climatologically, Long Island is much closer to these French wine regions than it is to California, and that fact gives the first clue to the general style of Long Island's wines.

Traditionally, particularly in France, soils are considered a key, and by some *the* key, to a wine's special character. Where do the mineral, flinty scents come from in the wines of Graves, Pouilly Fumé or Barolo, if not from the soils?

Some properties of the soil, such as drainage, can be of great importance in rainy areas such as Bordeaux and Long Island, while insignificant in areas with dry, hot summers such as California and Australia. When the roots of a vine absorb too much water, the flavors of the grapes are diluted and the skins can burst. Leaf growth is stimulated, grape clusters are shaded, ripening can be delayed and problems of fungal infection and rot become more pronounced. In the Long Island circumstance, adequate drainage is more of an issue than soil fertility, as are variations in vineyard slope, and the depth and extent of vine roots.

The nature of the soils of Long Island was determined some ten thousand years ago when, at the end of the last ice age, a retreating glacier sculpted Long Island. It is thought that the two forks of the Island's East End correspond to the two final advances of the Wisconsin glaciation. On the South Fork one can still see round depressions, or kettle holes, that are the imprints of slowly melting blocks of ice plowed under the surface by the glacial mass. The glacier thoughtfully left behind a soil that is virtually ideal for growing grapes in the current Long Island climate. It is sandy and coarse, with some loam, and is largely permeable to water. The driest soils tend to be on the tops of the hillocks that undulate gently across the landscape, and the wettest tend to be in the low lying areas. Different grapes have their favorite locales. Cabernet Sauvignon, for example, prefers the dryer knolls, while Merlot prefers the flat lands.

Because soil constituents can play a role in wine flavor, terroir can have a time dimension. Early on, some critics of Long Island wines claimed they could taste the residual flavors from the cauliflowers that were grown in the fields before vines were planted. In many of the great vineyards of Europe, yeast-laden, fermented skins have been returned to the soil year after year for centuries. The gradual build-up of nutrients from that special form of soil fertilization, and the symbiotic relationship with the wild yeasts that inhabit the soil, all contribute to the untold nuances of aroma in the wines of Burgundy and elsewhere. On Long Island, for the most part, winemakers rely on cultivated strains of commercial yeast that are trouble free, but which may restrict the palette of aromas. Over time, as Long Island vines have grown older, and as their roots have penetrated deeper into the earth, the relationships between vine and soil have changed. By now, many vines have reached maturity, while others are being planted each year. The relationships between vine and soil are complex and will continue to evolve.

The issue of terroir exists on various geographical scales, from the regional to the very local. On Long Island, because of the lack of hills and the geological uniformity of the soils, there are not the sharp vineyard-to-vineyard variations that exist in Burgundy or along the Rhine. There are, however, variations on two other scales. First, the topsoil that covers gravel and sand tends to be thin and subject to local erosion. Thus, in the lower areas of a given vineyard, the soil can be significantly richer and heavier than the higher, well drained, eroded soils. Several winemakers have by now identified the areas that tend to produce the most desirable grapes (which generally are the better drained areas) and selectively use those grapes for their premier wines.

Second, there are significant differences between the North and South Forks that lead to two designated regions, or Appelations: "North Fork of Long Island" and "The Hamptons, Long Island." The wine-producing region of the South Fork is an oblong of land roughly twenty miles long and seven miles wide. The Atlantic Ocean to the south takes the edge off winter temperatures and cools down the summer with ocean breezes. The predominant winds, however, are westerlies that pass over the main body of Long Island and a small stretch of Great Peconic Bay.

The North Fork is a narrow finger pointing in a more northerly direction than the South Fork, almost exactly to the northeast. At its thickest it is a mere five miles across. Long Island Sound lies to the west and north; the Peconic Bay to the south. If you stand on a beach half way out the North Fork and look due west, into the direction of the prevailing wind, you look straight down the Sound. The line of sight would hit land around the New York-Connecticut boundary, some fifty miles away. In contrast with the main body of Long Island, over which the South Fork breezes blow, the Sound in winter is a heat source. The North Fork's winds are preferentially warmed, yielding a slight, but significant temperature advantage.

A good measure of temperature as it affects the growing of grapes is the number of "growing-degree days." This is a measure of the extent to which temperatures exceed fifty degrees Fahrenheit over time. On the North Fork that number is about 3,000 while it is around 2,500 on the South Fork. More critical, perhaps, is the fact that on the North Fork, the last spring frost occurs around the beginning of April, while in the Hamptons it can be as much as three weeks later.

There are also significant differences of soil between the two Forks. Although soil composition can vary markedly within distances of ten or twenty feet, the soils of the South Fork tend to be richer, while those on the North Fork tend to be more gravelly and better drained. The combination of all of these differences gives the North Fork a decided edge, particularly for red grapes. As a result, some wines made at South Fork wineries are actually made from North Fork grapes. Other South Fork wines are made only from South Fork grapes, and thus can bear the Hamptons appelation.

Grapes grown in Nassau County at the Banfi estate are another matter, since the vineyards are inland and in a distinctive microclimate. Moreover, vinification takes place at a winery in upper New York State.

Terroir, of course, has no meaning independent of the grape varieties that are its product We now turn to the specific grapes that have been found to be most eloquent in expressing the Long Island terroir.

The Grapes of Long Island

There are recurrent discussions about the relative merits of the various species of grape vines, but either for reasons of tradition or of innate quality, one species, *Vitis vinifera*, has all but conquered the wine world. Vinifera vines, said to originate in East Asia, were brought to Europe from the area of the Caspian Sea. Virtually all the wines of Europe, certainly the finest wines, are made from vinifera grapes.

The grapes native to the United States, the Concord and Niagra, for example, belong to the *Vitis labrusca* species and historically formed the basis of many American wines. They have a characteristic flavor, however, often referred to as "foxy," that most people find undesirable in a wine. They could never produce wines of the distinction and subtlety that can be produced by Cabernet Sauvignon or Chardonnay. Unfortunately, some regions of the United States, including upstate New York, are simply too cold to produce wines from vinifera grapes on a reliable basis. Thus, tremendous efforts have been made to develop hybrids which combine vinifera qualities with labrusca hardiness. Indeed, the so-called French Hybrids were developed as early as the 1880s in France, not so much for their cold-hardiness, as for their resistance to the phylloxera louse. Even the hybrids, however, are no match for true vinifera varieties when noble wines are the objective.

Awaiting spring, Hargrave Vineyard.

Except for one ill-fated attempt to grow and sell Seyval Blanc, one of the finest French Hybrids, grape growers on Long Island have concentrated on vinifera grapes. Most of the most notable wines produced on Long Island are varietal wines. That is, they are predominantly made from a single vinifera grape variety. Federal law requires that a wine labelled with a varietal name contain at least seventy-five percent that grape.

In the following pages we introduce the principal grape varieties used on Long Island. These grapes tie the eastern end of Long Island to the great wine producing areas of the world.

The Whites

CHARDONNAY   Most Long Island winemakers (and wine lovers) would agree that Chardonnay is the premier Long Island white wine. The fact that Chardonnay has also been this country's fashionable white wine over recent years suggests that the priority given to it may have been based on market demand. However, the fact remains that the soils and climate of the region appear to be extraordinarily well suited to Chardonnay, and proof of that is in the bottles of many Long Island winemakers.

Chardonnay is a relatively easy grape to grow. It has been called forgiving, for it grows vigorously, has relatively high yield and is not damaged by Long Island's winter temperatures. Its major fault is that it can be fooled by a late winter warm spell into an early budding which is then susceptible to spring frosts.

In any event, Chardonnay was a logical bet for Long Island. The Chardonnay grape forms the basis of some of the best white wines of France. The white wines of Burgundy, for example, from Chablis at the region's northern tip, down through Montrachet in the Côte de Beaune, to Pouilly Fuissé in Southern Burgundy, are made almost exclusively from the Chardonnay grape. In Champagne, Chardonnay is usually combined with Pinot Noir and/or Pinot Meunier to produce that region's sparkling delights. Some excellent Champagne is also made from pure Chardonnay, and is usually labelled Blanc de Blanc (white wine from white grapes.) Vineyards from Chile to South Africa to Australia, not to mention California, now produce excellent Chardonnays to meet an apparently insatiable world market. It is even said that far more "Chardonnay" is drunk each year than is produced from Chardonnay grapes.

Although there is a great variety of wines produced throughout France with the Chardonnay grape, it is useful to distinguish the clean, tart, crisp wines characteristic of Chablis from the heavier, richer wines of Meursault or Montrachet. The differences are complex, but one crucial influence is the more common use of oak barrels for aging of the southern Burgundy wines. Chardonnay's varietal flavor is often muted, and the kind of oak, and its method of use, will have a strong influence on the character of the resulting wine. Indeed, one of the reasons winemakers like to make Chardonnay is that there are several factors under their control that can be used to craft the final product. Among these are the harvesting conditions, temperature of the first fermentation, whether or not a secondary fermentation is used and the use of oak .

One of the first serious efforts to make a Burgundy-style Chardonnay in California was by James Zellerbach at Hanzell Vineyards in the 1950s. Zellerbach was scrupulous not only in managing his vines, but also in using Limousin oak barrels for aging his wines. The success of the Hanzell Chardonnays was an important ingredient in establishing a California style of Chardonnay—rich, nutty, buttery and heavily oaked. Indeed, oak flavors predominate in many California Chardonnays to a much larger degree than in the white Burgundies that are their inspiration.

On Long Island, a wide range of Chardonnays is being produced. Although most winemakers use a malolactic fermentation (a secondary fermentation) to produce a rounder and softer wine, a few do not, preferring a brighter flavor. Several vineyards produce two Chardonnays. One may be designated as a Reserve or Estate Reserve which tends more to the California or Southern Burgundy style. The other is usually a straight

Chardonnay, fermented in stainless steel tanks, and which may have little or no oak aging. This produces a brighter, lighter wine more reminiscent of a Chablis or an Alsatian wine. The best grapes may also be used in the Reserve, and there may be other differences as well. One will certainly be that the Reserve will be more expensive. It is always interesting to taste different Chardonnays made by the same person in the same year, since the effects of specific choices are revealed. You may even prefer the standard variant over the fancier wine. It is a question of taste.

SAUVIGNON BLANC   There is considerable dispute about second place in the Long Island white wine hierarchy. This may reflect the market, for the American public is far less unanimous when considering anything beyond Chardonnay. It also reflects differences in taste and preference between the owners and winemakers themselves. Some are enthusiasts of Riesling or Gewürztraminer, while others consider Sauvignon Blanc to be the sleeper of Long Island whites.

The Sauvignon Blanc grape is grown across a broad band of Europe extending from Bordeaux on the Atlantic coast, through France and Northern Italy and into Yugoslavia, Bulgaria and Romania. However, it is Sancerre, a village clustered on a young breast of a hill above a bend in the Loire river that is the center of Sauvignon Blanc culture. It is there that the wines epitomize the fresh, clean character of the grape. The town may well have been the birthplace of Sauvignon Blanc, for it is said that the monks of a nearby abbey isolated the grape by careful, time-consuming selection in the Middle Ages.

In other parts of Europe Sauvignon Blanc is known by a variety of names. On the bank of the Loire opposite Sancerre is the village of Pouilly-sur-Loire. There the local name for the grape is Blanc Fumé, and the wine produced is the universally appreciated Pouilly-Fumé. In Bordeaux the Sauvignon Blanc grape teams with Semillon to produce an extraordinary range of white wines from unctuously sweet Sauternes, such as Château d'Yquem, to the rich, but dry whites of the Graves region.

In the United States, Robert Mondavi elevated Sauvignon Blanc from a grape misused in mediocre wines to the front rank by adding care and oak aging to the winemaking process. He called the resulting wines Fumé Blanc. On Long Island, Alex and Louisa Hargrave have used the name Blanc Fumé for their wine in homage to the enchanting Loire Valley wines.

At their purest, Sauvignon Blanc wines are full of fresh, tart aroma, sometimes with a whiff of peaches. They are zesty, refreshing wines with the best having an additional flinty or smoky (fumé) flavor and moderate depth. They are wines to be drunk well-chilled and young, within a couple of years of harvest.

Sauvignon Blanc takes naturally to the Long Island climate. However, particularly in a wet summer, it is prone to attack by botrytis and black rot. Its Achilles' heel is its vigorous vegetative growth through the end of the summer which makes the vine susceptible to winter injury. Vineyard managers tend to use both restricted trellis systems and severe hedging to control that growth.

In recent years, Bidwell and Jamesport, as well as Hargrave Vineyards, have produced fine examples of Long Island Sauvignon Blanc.

GEWÜRZTRAMINER Winemakers are generally an optimistic breed. They have to be or they would not survive the vicissitudes of the business. But even they can be discouraged. The odd hurricane that ravages a promising harvest can do it. So can Gewürztraminer. Many Long Island vintners produce lovely flavorful Gewürztraminers, but have great trouble selling them. The vintners say it is a public relations problem. The public does not understand the wine. Furthermore, they do not know how to pronounce it, and that is even more inhibiting. For the record, put the accent on "würz" and pronounce the "w" like a "v."

Although the Gewürztraminer grape is widely planted, it is in Alsace in France that it achieves its recognized identity. Gewürztraminer vies with Riesling for the place of honor in that region, and if Gewürztraminer takes second place, it is because of its own versatility. *Gewürz* means spice in German, and fine examples of the wine are always imbued with a flowery bouquet and a spiciness that accounts for its name. However, the wine can range from dry to sweet, and from light to high in alcohol, depending on the heat of the summer and the method of vinification. The classic Alsatian Gewürztraminer, however, is an enchanting combination of sweet, rose-scented aromas and a dry but complex taste.

On Long Island, Pat and Peter Lenz, the founders of The Lenz Winery made the first serious attempt to produce Gewürztraminer. Pat, a highly regarded chef, wanted to produce a wine that would complement the flavorful cuisine of the United States Southwest. They aimed at a fragrant, but dry style reminiscent of Alsatian wines, and it is that style that predominates among Long Island vintners today.

In principal, it should be easier to produce a classical Gewürztraminer on Long Island than in California. The hotter West Coast climate tends to increase sugars and lower acids with the result being a loss of varietal character and structure in the wine. The major hazard in growing the grape on Long Island is that the vines are subject to winter damage unless their natural, vigorous growth habits are carefully constrained in the latter part of the growing season.

Long Island Gewürztraminers are extremely likeable wines. Perhaps a little difficult to pair with food, but marvelous with a picnic, before dinner or with a curry or other spicy fare. A local connoisseur recommends Gewürztraminer with veal. The Lenz Winery continues to produce a Gewürztraminer, as does Palmer and Pindar Vineyards.

RIESLING Riesling is the grape of the finest wines of Germany, those produced along the Rhine and Mosel rivers. The grapes are sometimes called White or Johannisberg Riesling and, in the hands of German winemakers, form the basis of a marvelous spectrum of wines. On Long Island it is a controversial wine. Some winemakers such as Richard Olsen-Harbich of Bridgehampton, who apprenticed under a master Riesling maker, swear by it. Others say that Riesling is just not suited to Long Island's warm, wet summers. Although the vines are not fazed by Long Island winters, the grapes are prone to bunch rot during all too characteristic warm, wet periods. Some Riesling vines planted in the early eighties were even torn out at the end of the decade.

Part of the difficulty in selling Riesling is the impression of American wine drinkers, an impression based on an earlier California, rather than the German, version of the wine. The grape produces its greatest wines—crisp with beautiful, fruity aromas—in cooler climates. The heat of a California summer can wilt the structure of Riesling and produce a flabby, uninteresting wine. While there are now some fine Rieslings produced in California, particularly of the sweeter, late harvest variety, it is the high volume, mediocre wines that have given Riesling a bad name in this country. The winemakers of Washington, Oregon and upper New York State, however, are producing Rieslings of interest and integrity more in keeping with the German standards.

Whether Long Island, with its warm summers, can produce Rieslings of the highest quality on a consistent basis remains to be seen. There is already encouraging evidence from Palmer and Pindar Vineyards, Bidwell Vineyards and Bridgehampton Winery. If the Long Island Rieslings have thus far not had the depth of their models, they generally have been fresh and crisp wines with lovely floral bouquets characteristic of the variety. Recently, Paumanok Vineyards has produced both a dry Riesling and a popular, semi-sweet version.

Long Island winemakers have, when conditions were favorable, also produced worthy late harvest Rieslings. The Riesling grape is naturally high in acid and can be left on the vine much longer than other varieties to allow the sugars to build up. The phenomenon is pushed to its risky extreme in some German wines, where the grapes are traditionally harvested in December and even January (the *Dreikönigswein*). Some of these naturally sweet wines are the result of the workings of a fungus, *Botrytis cinerea*, sometimes called noble rot, which can attack grapes at the end of their growing season. Botrytis not only concentrates the sugar in the grapes by drying them out, but also adds a distinctive, earthy flavor. The first late harvest Riesling produced on Long Island was made by Richard Olsen-Harbich at Bridgehampton Vineyards. Nice examples have also been produced by Bidwell Vineyards and Bedell Cellars.

PINOT BLANC   Pinot Blanc, a clone of the red Pinot Noir, is a popular varietal in Alsace, northern Italy and recently, Oregon. The leaf clusters are sometimes difficult to distinguish from Chardonnay, and some early plantings on Long Island thought to be Chardonnay turned out to be Pinot Blanc. Turning disappointment to their advantage, at least one winery, on discovering Pinot Blanc in a newly acquired vineyard of "Chardonnay," adapted their vinification techniques to the imposter. The grape is about as versatile as Chardonnay to cultivate. The wines can be clean and smooth, often similar to Chardonnays, but without its depth of flavor. Both Hargrave and Palmer Vineyards produce attractive Pinot Blancs.

CHENIN BLANC   Chenin Blanc is hard to pin down, for the wines produced from the grape vary so widely around the world. It is extensively planted in South Africa, but the best known versions of Chenin Blanc are those from the Loire regions of Vouvray, Saumur and Anjou. It ripens very late and only then does it overcome its naturally high acidity. Its best expressions exhibit a floral bouquet and a texture that Rabelais associated with taffeta. On Long Island, Paumanok Vineyard produces a representative straightforward varietal.

The Reds

MERLOT   The name Merlot is sometimes associated with *merle*, the French word for blackbird, and the bird's ravenous taste for the grape gives the connection some credence. The emergence of Merlot as Long Island's premier red wine grape, and the public's taste for it, is a bit surprising. Cabernet Sauvignon would have been a more obvious choice because of its commercial appeal, and some maintain that Cabernet will win out in the long term. In the meanwhile, Merlot's ascendancy is an encouraging indication that the Long Island terroir is being allowed to direct the outcome of varietal experimentation in the region.

Merlot is a major constituent of many of the great wines of Bordeaux. In fact, in the greater Bordeaux region there is almost twice as much land planted in Merlot than in Cabernet Sauvignon. Many of the wines of Pomerol contain Merlot as the primary constituent. Château Pétrus, the district's most famous wine, and some would say Bordeaux's greatest, is usually made with one hundred percent Merlot grapes. In many of the vineyards of St. Emilion, where it is usually blended with Cabernet Franc, Merlot also predominates.

Merlot is grown widely in Europe, and seems to express itself best in a relatively northern climate. It produces fine wine in northern Italy, Switzerland, Yugoslavia and Hungary. It is now the fastest expanding variety in California.

The adjective that most often characterizes the quality given to a wine by the Merlot grape is softness. Wines made purely from Merlot mature quickly and can be enjoyed young, but, the great Pomerols not withstanding, they can be somewhat one-dimensional. While Merlots typically have generous fruit flavors, they often lack depth and complexity. After a typical summer, Merlot grapes will contain a high sugar level, but much lower tannins than Cabernet Sauvignon. On Long Island, it is thus common to blend some Cabernet Sauvignon (ten to twenty percent) to give a Merlot wine more backbone and complexity.

One of the greatest risks in growing Merlot results from one of the grape's otherwise desirable characteristics: its vigorous growth habits. After a cold winter, Merlot is raring to go in spring. An early warm spell can trigger the budding process, and if temperatures then return to below freezing, the buds can be killed. A related problem is *coulure*, a failure of flowers to develop. The vine is also susceptible to winter damage. Cold winters of 1984 and 1987 in Bordeaux killed forty- to fifty-year-old vines by the thousands. Nonetheless, in the Long Island climate, Merlot grapes attain an early, full ripeness and can be picked at whatever point the winemaker considers ideal.

Virtually all of the Long Island vineyards make a Merlot varietal wine, and many of these wines have been widely acclaimed. In good years, such as 1988, several vineyards may decide to bottle a special Merlot, often called a Reserve, as well as their standard bottling.

CABERNET SAUVIGNON   Bordeaux has an aura of nobility. With its venerable chateaux and its roots extending back to the first century A.D., it all but defines the culture of wine. Despite the sale of prominent châteaux to British and Japanese conglomerates, the region still bespeaks a natural aristocracy, in touch with the soil and with the finer things in life. From the days of Thomas Jefferson, American connoisseurs have taken the wines of Bordeaux as their standard of vinicultural quality. Although several grape varieties are used in Bordeaux wines, the most notable and characteristic is Cabernet Sauvignon.

Winemakers call it "Cab," and their affection for the grape is not surprising. It has all the qualities of a perfect friend. It has a strong and vivacious personality, is hale and hearty, and is reliable. Unlike Pinot Noir, for example, the trusty Cabernet Sauvignon flavors emerge under a wide range of growing conditions. Admittedly, like some of the most interesting older people, in its youth Cabernet Sauvignon can be objectionable: aggressive and overconfident. These personality traits derive from relatively large pips and thick skins which produce naturally strong tannins. The sharp edges of Cabernet's personality become smoothed by age, however, and in the best a marvelous medley of flavors emerges over time; flavors of vanilla, spice, black current and other fruits, as well as oak imparted by the casks in which the wine is fermented and stored.

In its youth pure Cabernet can be so awkward and take so long to mature that in most Bordeaux wines it is blended with softer grape varieties such as Cabernet Franc or Merlot. In response to impatient market forces, winemaking techniques are also being adjusted to produce Cabernets that are smoother earlier.

Although it can be grown under a wide range of conditions, Cabernet Sauvignon does require a high accumulation of heat during the summer to bring out its best. Some Bordeaux summers fall short and other grapes such as Cabernet Franc, whose quality varies less with temperature, are used as a partial replacement. Sugar must often be added in the fermentation process. On Long Island, while the summer temperatures are generally higher than in Bordeaux, many summers are not quite long enough to produce perfectly ripened grapes. Long Island winters are also more severe, and Cabernet Sauvignon vines can suffer as a result.

While Merlot may be the red wine grape for Long Island's present, there are those who believe that in the long run the best reds will be made from a blend, with Cabernet at its core. Pindar Vineyards, under the guidance of Dimitri Tchelistcheff, has made the most serious attempt thus far at producing a Bordeaux-style blended wine based on Cabernet Sauvignon. This wine, Mythology, incorporates Merlot, Cabernet Franc, Petit Verdot and, in some years, Malbec along with a base of Cabernet Sauvignon.

Most wineries on the Island produce a "Cab", often adding ten to twenty percent Merlot to soften the wine and make it accessible earlier. Palmer, Bedell and Lenz have all made Cabernets of superior quality. The Hargraves used the grape in their original planting. While some of their early bottlings were uneven, others, such as the 1980 Vintner's Signature Cabernet Sauvignon, have demonstrated that Long Island Cabernets can acquire Bordeaux-like complexity and integration with bottle age of over a decade.

Modern vinification techniques tend to accelerate the maturation of Cabernet based wines. However, experimentation with these wines is still a long term proposition and a low priority when cash flow is a major concern. Long Island is just beginning its evolution in this area, but the promise is great.

PINOT NOIR Many wine lovers and several winemakers on Long Island would agree with Alec Waugh when he wrote: "At the age of twenty I believed that the first duty of a wine was to be red, the second that it should be Burgundy. During forty years I have lost faith in much, but not in that." To many, the highest accomplishments of the winemaking art are the great red wines of Burgundy: Chambertin, La Tache, Clos de Vougeot, Richebourg and their brethren.

The Pinot Noir grape is the basis for all of these wines. No grape, however, is as elusive and difficult. In part this is because it exists in so many slight genetic variants and is so sensitive to growing conditions. Jancis Robinson describes Pinot Noir as "a minx of a vine...an exasperating variety for growers, winemakers and wine drinkers alike. It leads us a terrible dance, tantalizing with an occasional glimpse of the riches in store for those who persevere, yet obstinately refusing to be tamed." Over 200 clones of Pinot Noir have been identified in Burgundy alone. Two dozen varieties may contribute to a single wine. Some would say that this clonal variety is one of the secrets of the subtle complexity of the great Burgundies.

Pinot Noir leads a double life, for in addition to producing celestial red wines, it is also a primary constituent of the great sparkling white wines of Champagne. In that role it is often blended with some combination of Chardonnay, Pinot Meunier or Pinot Blanc. Unless a pink Champagne is desired, the skins are removed from the juice immediately after the black grapes are crushed.

On Long Island, pure red wines from Pinot Noir are more of a dream than a reality. A major problem is the Long Island climate. The close packing of the grapes in the cluster makes Pinot Noir highly susceptible to bunch rot in such a damp climate. It was one of the original grape varieties planted by the Hargraves and at Lenz Winery. They both make Pinot Noir wines from time to time. Gristina Vineyards also produces small amounts of Pinot Noir from their grapes. Others, such as Palmer Vineyards and Mattituck Hills Winery, have used Pinot Noir to make rosé wines by allowing the naturally white juice to have only brief contact with the skins. Both Pindar and Lenz have used Pinot Noir in sparkling wines.

Whether Long Island ever produces a notable Pinot Noir remains to be determined, but we doubt whether the winemakers will ever give up the search. Pinot Noir devotees will just have to be patient. After all, by the time Louis IV became devoted to their wines, the Burgundians had been experimenting with the best combination of grape variety, location and winemaking technique for well over a thousand years.

CABERNET FRANC   If, as a youngster, you had an annoyingly successful, smart and popular older brother or sister, you know how Cabernet Franc must feel. As the younger sister to Cabernet Sauvignon, Cabernet Franc is often not given the respect she deserves. Why should Cabernet Sauvignon get all the publicity? It is true that the older brother is more assertive and bold (older brothers are always full of acid and tannin,) but the younger sister has some exceptional qualities of her own. Her voice is softer and she wears delicate perfumes. As a youngster she is much more approachable. In some ways, beneath the surface, she is stronger than her older brother. For example, she gets through a cold winter in much better shape. The delight, though, is that when the brother and sister play together constructively, they bring out each other's best.

While less prevalent than thirty years ago, Cabernet Franc is still one of the major grape varieties of Bordeaux. It is usually a minor (ten to twenty percent) partner, but in St. Emilion it often plays a major role. Château Cheval Blanc, often referred to as the quintessential St. Emilion wine, is normally about two thirds Cabernet Franc. Like Merlot, it is used to soften the hard edges of Cabernet Sauvignon, and contributes its own complexity and floral bouquet. There is sometimes a spicy or briary flavor to Cabernet Franc wines; Robert Parker detects a "weedy, olive-like aroma," while Jancis Robinson is reminded of the aroma of pencil shavings. This is sounding less and less like something one would be inclined to drink.

Nevertheless, in the Loire region Cabernet Franc is a favored red wine grape, being used for the reds of Bourgueil and Chinon, for example. That region's best rosés, particularly from Anjou, are also made from this flexible variety. In northern Italy the grape is even more popular than its more famous older brother, presumably because it produces a wine that is ready to drink sooner after harvest. In California, Cabernet Franc is widely used, but usually as a minor partner to the older brother, rather than as a pure varietal wine.

Cabernet Franc is being given the chance to stand on its own on Long Island by several wineries including Palmer, Pindar, Paumanok and Hargrave. Richard Olsen-Harbich, the winemaker at Bridgehampton Winery, where some of the first Cabernet Franc were planted, points out that the variety produces a wine that ripens much earlier than Cabernet Sauvignon (around the time that Chardonnay is picked) and produces a softer wine that can be drunk earlier. In most years, while their precocious sisters have

Bottling sparkling wine, méthode champenoise, *Pindar Vineyards*.

already been picked, destemmed and crushed, clusters of Cabernet Sauvignon are still out on the vines trying to ripen under the last rays of summer sun. Yes, the older brother always gets the good deal.

Other Wines

By a wide margin, most of the wine produced on Long Island is varietal, based on one of the grape varieties discussed above. There are other kinds of wine, however, that the visitor may well encounter. These non-varietal or blended wines fall into three categories. The first is the premium quality red wine, blended from a mix of grapes, as is done by the great châteaux of Bordeaux. The grapes are usually fermented separately and then, after several months of barrel aging, are combined in the proportions that the winemaker feels is the most propitious. Pindar Vineyards' Mythology is the oldest version of this classical wine form which, in the United States, is sometimes referred to as Meritage. Bridgehampton also produces a Reserve, made from Cabernet Sauvignon and Cabernet Franc.

Sparkling wines constitute the second category of non-varietal wines produced on Long Island. The controversy over what can and cannot be called Champagne has been raging for decades over dinner tables and in the international courts. The French consider that only sparkling wine from specified regions of the province called Champagne (made from certain kinds of grapes according to specified techniques) should be able to bear that magic name. We accept that position, not in support of French chauvinism, but in admiration of the quality of Champagne from Champagne. Wines that are made using the traditional method, in which the secondary fermentation occurs in the bottle, are referred to as *méthode champenoise* sparkling wines. An alternative and less expensive method, developed in 1907 by Eugene Charmat, carries out the secondary fermentation in tanks. These wines are referred to as Charmat or bulk process sparkling wines. Sparkling wines can be made from a variety of grapes. Those made only from white grapes, often Chardonnay, are called Blanc de Blanc.

Disgorging sediment, Pindar Vineyards.

An increasing number of Long Island wineries have been attracted to the making of sparkling wine, all in the traditional méthode champenoise. Both Lenz Winery and Pindar Vineyards use a combination of red and white grapes. Pindar has also made a pink sparkling wine and an unusual Cuvée Rare sparkling wine from Pinot Meunier grapes. Pugliese Vineyards makes a Blanc de Blanc sparkling wine, as does Villa Banfi. In the latter case the Chardonnay grapes are grown at the vineyard in Old Brookville, and the wine is vinified in upstate New York.

The third category of non-varietal Long Island wines covers a broad spectrum. These wines are often made from young vines, usually fermented and aged in steel rather than oak, and are often designed to be enjoyed sooner than their pampered peers. Pampering is expensive, so the non-varietals are usually considerably cheaper than their high class counterparts.

The vagaries of nature, combined with the skill and natural inventiveness of Long Island winemakers, often produce interesting results. Hurricane Bob ripped through the North Fork in September of 1991 doing scattered damage to the vineyards. Hargrave Vineyard's Hurricane Bob Candlelight Burgundy appeared early in 1992 carrying a label that told the story: "Clusters of this wine hung tenaciously on the vine during eighty mile an hour winds that stripped many leaves but none of the fruit. So well engineered are grapes that they will not quit hanging on until they are good and ready to be picked. We gathered them into the calm of the cellar letting the wine calmly recollect the beauty of the season that preceded it." The resulting wine was charming, with the soft lightness of a well made Beaujolais and delicate but clear Burgundian flavors of the Pinot Noir grapes from which it was made.

Kip Bedell is another inventive sort. Several years ago he noticed that the fungus, *Botrytis cinerea,* had attacked a portion of his Chardonnay vineyard. Taking his cue from the sweet wines of Sauterne, where botrytis is allowed to dry out and intensify the sugar in grapes at the end of their ripening, Kip produced an intense, deeply sweet, late harvest wine; a highly unusual form of Chardonnay. On another occasion, visitors were drawn into Kip's cellar by a tantalizing, jammy aroma to find Kip fermenting a wine from freshly picked raspberries. Those fortunate enough to visit Long Island's vineyards, shouldn't neglect these "one-off" wines. Generally they are only available at the vineyard, and, in these days of increasing uniformity in winemaking methods, they bring a special pleasure to the wine lover.

From Grapes to Wine

Before there were wineries on Long Island, there must have been visions of vines clinging to trellises in long rows of verdant foliage, of attractive oak casks neatly stacked in a cool cellar and of bins upon bins of bottles with pretty labels: the ultimate expression of a proprietor's whimsy. A vast chasm stretches between these visions and their attainment, however. Years of nurturing and waiting, of financial investments that may never become profitable, of doubt and uncertainty, and of learning on the job await the new vineyard management. Despite new evidence of winemaking in Mesopotamia five millennia ago, there is still no foolproof prescription for a successful vineyard. The Long Island winemaker must make countless decisions throughout the seasons, but the net result of those decisions does not appear in the bottle for some years.

The first critical decision leading to a successful winery is the selection of the vineyard site. This is arguably the most important factor in determining the quality of the grapes and the yield of a vine. Our earlier discussion pointed out that different fates await grapes that grow in sunny elevated sites with good drainage, as opposed to those that grow in the more poorly drained and cooler areas. Water and cold air tend to collect wherever the landscape is depressed. This can lead to an excessive proliferation of vines during the growing season and to an increased risk of killing frosts in winter. Moreover, deposits of silt and non-porous materials from an adjacent hill can build up in a gully. This exacerbates the poor drainage of bottom sites. On the other hand, if a slope is too steep, the water available to a vine planted there is drastically reduced.

One Long Island vineyard owner was plagued for over ten years with an ill-chosen site, before he tore out acres of vines and moved elsewhere. Perhaps it took the unfortu-

Extending bird netting, Pellegrini Vineyards.

nate owner so long to admit the site's inadequacy because of year to year shifts in weather. Even a poor site can produce decent wine in favorable years. Perhaps it was the natural reluctance to give up on a vineyard that has cost so many dollars and taken so much effort to develop. Whatever the case, as Alex Hargrave once said, "The most creative act is where the winemaker plants his grapes."

Another consideration in choosing a site are the flocks of migratory birds that move across Long Island. If the vineyard is surrounded by woods and shrubs—good roosting areas—the risk of bird damage is increased. Especially troublesome has been the voracious starling. Charming in small numbers, these migratory birds become a dark, Hitchcockian menace as they sweep down in flocks of thousands, just as the grapes are reaching their ripe perfection. They can devour or spoil acres of ripe grapes in a matter of hours.

Long Island vineyard owners have tried all kinds of weapons in this battle: propane cannons, four-wheel, all-terrain vehicles, miles of shiny mylar tape, hawks, party balloons, and netting. Gristina Vineyards tried what is perhaps the most unusual defense. For a while, a young man by the name of Jeff Morgan worked for Gristina as marketing and sales director. Jeff was also a classical and jazz musician who wielded his saxophone in the annual war against the attacking flocks. It's not that he played badly; in fact he played very well, but he found that be-bop and certain kinds of free jazz, "free and fast arpeggiated lines," were particularly noisome to Gristina's feathered enemies.

In 1989 and 1990 the bird problem seemed to be getting worse and worse. Many vineyards, including Gristina, concluded that the only solution was to put netting over the entire vineyard during periods of bird migration. By then Jeff Morgan had moved on to become a respected wine reporter, but some say that on still and moonless nights, they can hear echoes of plaintive saxophone rambles floating through the Gristina vineyard.

A second critical decision, closely related to the issue of site selection, is the choice of grape variety. That choice has become increasingly easy over the years as experience has been gained on how different varietals have fared in the vineyard, and how the wines fared in the bottle. Some, like Cabernet Sauvignon, exhibit vigorous growth and so are best planted on lighter, more elevated soils, while others, such as Chardonnay, adapt to the drainage conditions found on a plateau. By now, any newcomer to the wine-making fraternity can draw on the accumulated wisdom of the other vineyard managers and winemakers. However, key uncertainties still remain, many of which revolve around marketing issues. In five years will there be a market for another Chardonnay? Can we really make a Riesling that will be accepted? Can we charge enough for a sparkling wine to make it worthwhile?

Hidden enemies of the vineyard manager are the fungi that attack the roots of the vines. Others are more apparent, such as the many forms of molds that attack the grapes themselves. Given its damp climate, Long Island would not be successful in growing vinifera grapes were it not for chemical sprays to prevent rot. Some fear that the continued use of such sprays may allow the fungi and molds to develop immunity that in time will increase the vulnerability of the vines to further attack.

The possible degradation of the underground aquifers that are infiltrated by these pesticides is also a concern. Needless to say, the federal Environmental Protection Agency provides regulations that are monitored regularly to protect fragile groundwater supplies, but the concern remains. Other voices are heard arguing that prime winemaking areas such as Bordeaux have lived with damp, disease-ridden, climatic conditions for several hundred years and are still prospering.

Perhaps the answer lies in alternate strategies for vineyard management, such as new trellising methods, or more careful canopy management that allows sunshine and cooling breezes to offset the harm done by humidity. Also, recent advances in genetic engineering, lead by the University of California at Davis and the French Champagne mogul, Moët, have produced disease resistant vines which may reduce chemical use in the long term. Related to this is the choice of rootstock. Experiences in California indicate a revival of phylloxera, a tiny louse that attacks the root system and withers the vine. This scourge affects a substantial fraction of the acreage planted in California and necessitates replanting with rootstock resistant to the pest. Long Islanders are keeping a wary eye on this possible affliction which, to date, does not appear to have penetrated the region.

One enemy that is practically unique to Long Island is the hurricane. It is an enemy of huge power for which there are no defenses, and it tends to attack at the vineyards' most vulnerable period, just before harvest. In late August of 1991, for example, Hurricane Bob roared through Long Island, with the eye passing over the eastern tip. While some vineyards were essentially unaffected, others, such as Jamesport Vineyards, suffered sufficient damage that they decided to pick their Chardonnay before the bruised grapes spoiled on the vine. The Hargraves made the same decision, not because of physical damage, but because the spray carried on the post-storm winds left slight salt deposits on the grapes that they feared would lead to damage. Hurricanes evidently breed a kind of resourcefulness that is special to Long Island winemakers.

Following site selection, the future viticulturist must prepare the land for planting by removing weeds and shrubs as well as trees, large rocks, and other obstructions, prior to plowing the field. Soil pH must be adjusted to a neutral value of about six by liming, since most of the uncultivated soils on the North Fork are fairly acidic.

Winter pruning, Banfi Vineyards.

Then the trellis is installed, with its vine supporting poles and wires. Next, the young vines are planted in rows running generally north-south to enhance sun exposure and reduce shading in the leaf canopy. At sufficient maturity, anywhere from three to four years after planting, the first grapes are harvested.

Conventional wisdom has it that only mature vines, whose roots have penetrated deep into the soil, and whose vigor of foliage and shoots is limited by age, can make a great wine. This is so because the less prolific vine can concentrate its growth on the few remaining grape clusters that now benefit from the attention they receive. However, the noted British wine authority, Clive Coates, affirms that although it is no doubt true that older vineyards, thirty to fifty years old perhaps, produce superior wine, there are exceptions, such as the 1961 Pétrus. That legendary wine was made from very young vines. He argues that a five year old vine produces a small number of grapes like an old vine does. Thereafter the vines become more exuberant and need to be tamed.

There are annual vineyard rituals that are familiar to grape growers the world around. During the late winter or early spring, when the vines have shed their foliage and lie dormant, the Long Island growers emerge to prune back the straggly and tangled mass to permit just a few pre-nascent buds to remain on the branches. At the same time, some of the slender canes of the vines are repositioned and tied to the trellis wires. Later in the spring, after bud-break and when the first clusters of fruit have set, any excessive leaf growth is pruned away and unwanted shoots at the base of the trunk are "suckered" or clipped away. During the summer a grower may remove some of the grape clusters in an attempt to concentrate the vines' vigor on the remaining crop. This reduces the yield at harvest, of course, but it also augments the color and extract of the grapes that remain. It is a trade-off between quality and quantity.

As much as possible the grower attempts to expose the fruit to sunlight and cleansing breezes. The goal is to obtain healthy and mature grape berries before harvest. After *veraison,* when the grapes take on their pigment—usually in August—the sugar levels begin to increase and the acidity starts to drop as the fruit ripens. For most grape varietals there is an optimum level of acid and sugar that cannot always be achieved in Long Island, especially in a growing season beset by too much rainfall, cloudy days and cool temperatures. Some growers try to offset this by picking late, during the usually more favorable autumn weather, and by practicing severe crop thinning during the summer. Other preventive measures may be necessary, such as vine spraying to counter attacks of rot and fungal diseases. Ultimately, it is the experience and commitment of the grower whose care in the vineyard determines the quality of the wine that goes into the bottle. Each year brings new climatic conditions to reckon with, and the grower copes with it by a combination of vigilance and hopeful expectancy, not to say prayers to Dionysian gods.

Harvest usually begins in mid to late September and may continue into October, depending on the season and the grape variety (some ripen earlier.) The prudent grower will examine each vine before picking and will drop all clusters of grapes that show signs of spoilage and immaturity, leaving on the vine the ripest and healthiest bunches.

At harvest time some of the most agonizing decisions must be made. The early-ripening grape varieties, such as Chardonnay, achieve the desired balance between sugar and acid content by early September and can be picked at a deliberate pace. However, a few days of unexpected rain will upset the balance and dilute the grapes' intensity of flavor. For others, such as Cabernet Sauvignon, few summers seem long enough, and the vineyard manager will attempt to leave the grapes on the vine as long as possible to benefit from the last warm, sunny days of Fall. It is a risky gamble, however. A deep killing frost can sneak in, or a hurricane can roar by to destroy whole vineyards of precious grapes. Picking too early may require the addition of sugar to the juice before fermentation, or a missed opportunity to make a better wine. Picking too late can mean deteriorated grapes, and an opportunity missed on the other side. It is a decision to which the winemaker, the vineyard manager, and the owner each brings his own expertise, but which must finally be made by the owner.

If the decision of when to pick is sometimes preceded by sleepless nights, it is always followed by days of intense work that leave little time for sleep. When the time has come to harvest on Long Island, more often than not a mechanical harvester will rumble through the lanes between the vines, prying them loose. In some instances the removal of grape clusters is done by hand by a team of pickers. This is time consuming and is certainly the more expensive way to harvest, but, depending on who you talk to, it is the only way to select grapes. Hand sorting reduces the chance of picking up unwanted debris and leaves, or under-ripe or moldy grape bunches. It also handles the vine itself more gently. It is the way harvesting is still done at the celebrated estates of Bordeaux, and at many of the front rank wine properties throughout Europe. Yet the advocates of mechanical harvesting claim that little or no harm is done to the vines, and that grapes arriving

Chardonnay grapes before…and after mechanical harvesting, Pindar Vineyards.

at the winery are indistinguishable from those obtained by the more arduous hand picking method. On Long Island both procedures are practiced and the jury is still out.

Each vineyard acre averages about 600 vines, which translates into about 3,000 bottles of wine. This yield varies with the density of plantings, the spacing between rows, the vigor of the grape variety and the severity of pruning in the months prior to harvest. Generally, higher quantity means lower quality.

As the vines get older they lose their vigor, and eventually, after twenty five or more years, some fraction of older vines must be replanted. This hasn't happened on Long Island as yet, but replacement of dead or diseased vines is not an uncommon occurrence even now. New vines can be grafted to existing root stocks, or the entire plant may need to be taken up, and a new vine planted.

Most Long Island wineries are equipped with mechanical devices called crusher-stemmers that, true to their word, crush the arriving batches of whole grapes to release the sugary pulp within, and separate the grape berry from stems and leaves. The crushed red wine grapes flow into stainless steel tanks in which the fermentation takes place. Fermentation is a magical time when the sugar in the juice is transformed into alcohol in the presence of certain species of yeasts. The activity begins a few hours after the grape juice enters the tanks and can last several days until all, or virtually all, the sugar has been converted. Vast quantities of heat are released, as well as carbon dioxide that escapes through the top of the tank. One can hear the bubbling and sizzling, and a beguiling odor emerges.

Long Island vintners generally use cultivated yeasts purchased from laboratories which they then inoculate into the grape juice. Although these yeasts are selected to ensure trouble free fermentations, a few winemakers are experimenting with a mixture of yeasts, including some wild strains. It is known that many of the flavors and aromas in a wine are the result of the specific action of yeasts on the fermenting juice. Different yeasts can enhance some aromas while reducing others, thereby allowing the winemaker to enlarge the color palette of the wine. This is a technique to be used with caution, however, since certain wild yeasts can give the wine unpleasant odors, and may even inhibit the positive action of other yeasts.

In the middle of the last century, the scientist Louis Pasteur gave the first rudimentary explanation of fermentation by implicating micro-organisms as catalysts. Significantly, lack of that knowledge did not impede previous generations in their winemaking. What happens during fermentation requires little intervention except for an occasional nudge and some corrective action here and there. For example, if the temperature in the tank is too high or low (fermentation works properly only within a certain range) the winemaker can correct it by cooling the tanks or heating the cellar. On Long Island, as elsewhere around the world, a few winemakers have invested in temperature controlled fermentation tanks to reduce the element of chance.

While fermentation proceeds, the juice is pumped over the cap of solid matter that has floated to the top in order to extract more color and flavor. When it is complete, the tanks are sealed to prevent spoilage of the wine by acetic bacteria in the air that convert the alcohol into vinegar. For certain wines, mostly reds, a second fermentation is allowed to take place in which other strains of bacteria act to convert the tart malic acids in the wine into the softer lactic acid, while also reducing overall acidity. This malolactic fermentation is a desirable change in that it can make a wine more supple and less biting. It is routinely practiced on Long Island for many of the Merlot and Cabernet Sauvignon wines and for some Chardonnays.

After fermentation has been completed, the detritus in the tank is allowed to settle out, and the clear liquid is pumped to a new tank or, depending on the wine, into wood barrels where the aging process begins. Before that occurs, the pumice at the bottom of the tank, consisting largely of grape skins, is gently pressed to squeeze out some the juice that is trapped in the mass. This is carried out in another mechanical device appropriately called a presser. On Long Island this press wine is usually, though not always, added to the other juice to add more body and color. This is done with some care in order to avoid a certain harshness of flavor that comes from the tannin in the skins and pits. For white wines this pressing is done at the beginning, not long after crushing, to avoid long skin contact that would color the wine too deeply.

When, in the judgement of the winemaker, the new wine has reposed sufficiently in its tank or barrel, it is ready to be filtered of impurities and clarified prior to bottling. The wines destined for aging may be given more time in wood than others in order to allow certain gradual, chemical reactions to take place. With time, complexity is added to the finished product. Oak, in particular, has a notable effect on the flavor of the wine and, used with moderation, enhances the fruit aromas of the grapes. The barrel staves are generally toasted by the supplier, to a lesser or greater degree, and this charring can impart certain smoky vanillin flavors to the finished wine. At present the main supplier of wood barrels on Long Island is the French firm of Sequin Moreau which uses oak from Limousin, Nevers, Troncais, and Alliers, each of which has its adherents. However, in any given cellar an assortment of other barrels may be found, including less expensive containers of uncharred American white oak.

These wood nuances can be exaggerated, however, and, although wood aging is commonplace on Long Island, it is one place where the winemaker's good sense must come into play.

Another critical activity is that of blending. Wines from different parts of a vineyard are sometimes fermented separately, as are the different varietals. After aging is completed, the individual vats are tasted to determine which, if any, should be blended together, and in what proportions. The idea is that the whole may be better than its constituent parts, and it may be that a blend of Cabernet Sauvignon, Cabernet Franc and Merlot is a more harmonious entity than a wine made from any one of the grapes alone. One varietal lends tannic backbone and firmness, another suppleness and seductive aromas, and a third provides certain spicy, exotic highlights, just as baritone, tenor and alto voices enrich each other while harmonizing in a choral group. Sometimes a solo voice is more compelling, however, and so it is that a wine made mainly from a single grape type may convey a richness and texture that is satisfying by itself.

From a marketing point of view, the blends are more problematic for Long Island vintners, since it is not clear what to call them. The public recognizes the name Cabernet Sauvignon, but it might shun a hybrid product with which it is unfamiliar. The red wines of Bordeaux are in fact blends, but the consumer has come to know them by the name of the estate or the commune in which the grapes are grown, rather than by the varietal name. Eventually the North Fork appellation may shift a wine's repute away from grape type towards place of origin.

Once the wine has been pumped into sterile bottles and corked, another machine regulated task, the labels are put on and the wines stored in cool facilities. The job of promotion, sales, and distribution can now begin.

Some Long Island wineries are fortunate in having several accomplished artisans who daily exercise their skill in a multitude of tasks, from vineyard management to nursing the wine into being in the cellar. The same technical experts may counsel several wineries, not unlike the midwifes of earlier times. Sometimes the winemaker is the owner, a double jeopardy where judgment in matters large and small shape the final product and may give the wine a competitive edge over a similar wine made by another producer. It is one of the delights of the consumer to recognize the shades of difference between wineries and to give the palm in each vintage to the more striking wine.

After a nineteenth century Long Island wine label.
(Courtesy of Mrs. Prescott B. Huntington)

CHAPTER 3

The Historical Legacy

*"…we must endeavor to make everything we want within ourselves,
and have as little intercourse as possible with Europe in its present
demoralized state. Wine being one of the earliest luxuries in which we
indulge ourselves, it is desirable that it should be made here,
and we have every soil, aspect and climate of the
best wine countries."*

—Thomas Jefferson, 1811

There are few commercial activities in the modern world in which history plays a larger role than in winemaking. The fabric of winemaking on Long Island, youthful and dynamic as it is, incorporates strands from many regions and past eras. The basic structure of the soils of Long Island was determined by the great workings of the Wisconsin ice sheet at the end of the last ice age. For many hundreds of years this land and the fertile waters surrounding it have rewarded the efforts of Native Americans, early European settlers and modern farmers.

The vines that grow so robustly in Long Island's soil have ancient lineages as well. Their core genetic structure probably evolved in the Transcaucasus area south of the Black Sea, but their specific characteristics result from their nurture by ancient Greeks, Etruscans, Romans and Gauls, as well as the Cistercian monks of medieval Burgundy and centuries of vineyardists in Bordeaux, Alsace and the other great wine regions of Europe.

There are some novel vineyard and vinification practices being used on Long Island. But often an innovation is merely a new juxtaposition of traditional techniques: a vinification technique typical of Germany, for example, being used for grapes traditionally grown in Bordeaux. If they visited a modern Long Island winery, Thomas Jefferson or Dom Pérignon, after tramping through the vineyard, ducking into the cellar, and asking a few incisive questions, would understand the system completely. They might even have a good suggestion or two.

The artifacts of wine consumption also participate in a lengthy historic tradition. Modern wine glasses would appear dull compared to their first century Roman predecessors. In the eighteenth century, the cork-stopped bottle evolved, much in the same shape as we know it today. At the same time, fortunately, some unknown genius invented the corkscrew, that indispensable device that allows us to unlock ancient legacies and pour the sunshine of a summer past into our expectant glass.

The Early Days

The history of winegrowing in America begins with the earliest European settlers. The story has as one of its dominant themes the competition between native American grapes and the imported vinifera varieties. Despite countless attempts in virtually all the colonies, no one seemed able to make acceptable wine from the native varieties. They ripened with too little sugar, too high acid levels and a "foxy" taste that most people found objectionable. There were always a few proud advocates of the native varieties. John Adlum, a viticulturist who died in 1836, is a good example. Referring to the Catawba grape, he declared, "In bringing this grape into public notice I have rendered my country a greater service than I could have done had I paid off the national debt." Of course, in those days the national debt didn't amount to much either.

Time and time again American wine lovers, including George Washington and Thomas Jefferson, expended prodigious efforts to import and grow European grape varieties, only to see their vineyards die away after a few promising harvests due to local diseases and pests. Around 1740, an accidental hybrid, a cross between a native vine and an imported vinifera, was discovered along the Schuylkill river near an abandoned vineyard of European grapes. The discoverer was James Alexander, gardener to the son of William Penn, and the Alexander grape was to become the first of many successful French-American hybrids. Despite some success of the hybrids, American growers continued to import European varieties in an attempt to emulate European wines.

One of the most controversial chapters in the history of American winemaking concerns the origins of Zinfandel, sometimes called California's mystery grape. Some equate Zinfandel with the Primitivo grape grown in southern Italy and trace its roots to the eastern Mediterranean. Another school firmly identifies Zinfandel as one of the grapes brought to this country by the legendary Count Agoston Haraszthy, who is known as the "Father of California Viticulture." In one popular account, Haraszthy first had Zinfandel vines shipped to California from his native Hungary in 1852. A fatal flaw in that account is that there is no mention of a Zinfandel-like grape in Hungarian ampelographies of the time, nor has there been any since.

Another problem with the theory of the 1852 introduction of Zinfandel to this country is that a Long Island nurseryman, William Prince, was growing Zinfandel at least as early as 1830. Prince advertised "Black Zinfardel" [sic] for sale in his catalog of that year. There has even been speculation that the Zinfandel clone, Primitivo, known in nineteenth century Italy as an imported variety, could have been brought to Italy from America, conceivably from Long Island.

Long Island's Early Wines

William Robert Prince was the most notable precursor of Long Island's current grape growers and winemakers. Prince was a fourth generation nurseryman and operated the Linnæan Botanic Garden in Flushing (in Queens County), popularly known as Prince Nurseries. In 1830 he published *A Treatise on the Vine* which contained a history of vinegrowing since Noah, instructions on vineyard practices and a description of 280 varieties of grapes, many of them vinifera. The treatise was by far the most authoritative work on the subject published to that date in this country. Prince also made wine from several grape varieties, but they were apparently not for public sale. In 1829, Prince published his discovery that a spray of a lime-sulfur mixture was effective against *oidium*, a common mildew. Unfortunately, that treatment was not effective against black rot and downy mildew, which eventually destroyed his vinifera vines. Those blights would not be conquered until 1885 with the discovery of Bordeaux mixture, a combination of copper sulfate and lime.

While the most prominent, Prince was not the only serious wine grape grower on Long Island in the nineteenth century. One of the most successful hybrid grapes he sold, the Isabella, was developed on Long Island by Colonel George Gibbs, who named it after his wife. In the early days of the century, Alphonse Loubat cultivated a vineyard of some forty acres along what is now the Brooklyn waterfront, and André Parmentier conducted extensive vinicultural experiments at the corner of Jamaica and Flatbush Avenues in Brooklyn. Both of their efforts were based on vinifera varieties, however, and were doomed to failure.

Further out on Long Island, at least by the 1870s, there was a successful vineyard and winery on the western shore of Stony Brook Harbor in what is now the Village of Nissequogue. According to the 1879 records of the Town of Smithtown, when Thomas Seabury sold his estate, Rassepeage, "extensive vineyards, the most complete collection of choice wine grapes in New York State," were included in the sale. The new owner, a Mr. Ruszits, built a separate wine cellar building, and his Rassepeage Claret was highly reputed.

The early nineteenth century also saw new vineyards planted north of New York City along the Hudson River. Vines had been planted in New Palz as early as 1677 by French Huguenot settlers. In 1839 a Frenchman named Jean Jaques established a vineyard and winery at Washingtonville. In the 1870s its name was changed to the Brotherhood Winery, and it continues to make wine to this day, the oldest winery in continuous operation in the country.

Native American grapes, and then the French-American hybrids, were the basis for a burgeoning grape and wine industry in the far western part of the state, and in the Finger Lakes region between Pennsylvania and Lake Ontario. The driving forces behind the New York State wine industry in this period were often French and German immigrants fleeing political turmoil in Europe. These promising efforts were hobbled, however, by the onset of Prohibition in 1919.

By the time Prohibition was repealed in 1933, the U.S. wine industry was in a shambles. Lucie Morton, author of *Wine Growing in Eastern America*, comments, "Wine was viewed as either too lowbrow for respectable households or so esoteric that you had to speak French in order to understand it." Over the next two decades, that gap was bridged in the eastern United States by the efforts of a few wine importers, writers and winemakers, such as Frank Schoonmaker, Philip Wagner, Charles Fournier and Konstantin Frank. Of particular importance to the story of Long Island wines is Dr. Frank, a viticulturist and enologist who was born in Russia to German parents. Frank ran a vinicultural research institute in Russia and, after the second world war, worked for the American occupation forces in Germany on agricultural projects. Eventually, in 1951 he and his family made their way to New York, arriving there with forty-one dollars between them.

As soon as he had saved a few more dollars, earned by washing dishes, Frank headed for the nearest wine region: New York's Finger Lakes district. He was determined to make wine there from vinifera grapes, despite two centuries of evidence that that was an impossible dream. Starting in the position of an unskilled vineyard hand, he eventually persuaded Charles Fournier to back his efforts. To much shaking of heads, Frank planted Riesling and Gewürztraminer vines. In his 1961 vintage, Frank produced a Riesling Trockenbeerenauslesen that caused a sensation. Made from hand selected grapes shriveled by botrytis rot, the naturally sweet wine sold for the unprecedented price of forty-five dollars a bottle, more than Frank had in his pocket when he arrived in this country ten years before.

Konstantin Frank, through his demonstration that vinifera grapes could be grown in the eastern United States, through his influence on the next generation of New York winemakers, and through visits to Long Island, had a profound influence on the Island's wine future. His name will come up several times as the story of Long Island wines unfolds.

The East End

The earliest European settlers of the East End of Long Island were mostly English and came from New England rather than New York. This might seen odd until one realizes that Montauk Point is closer to Boston than to Manhattan and that, in the seventeenth century, travel by sea was often easier than by land. The aptly named Shelter Island was settled at the end of the seventeenth century by Quakers from New England fleeing persecution.

The East End gradually became a flourishing agricultural region, but there is only incomplete evidence of early wine production. There are intriguing stories of a Moses "The Frenchman" Fournier growing grapes in Cutchogue as early as 1640, with the aid of the local Indians. Some claim that he even grafted French varieties onto native vines. A history of Cutchogue by Wayland Jefferson mentions that his "great vineyards were an outstanding feature of the town" in the early eighteenth century. However, Louisa Hargrave, in her historical research, could find no mention of a Fournier in the Southold Town records for that period and suggests that his vineyards were in fact on the South Fork.

Certainly by the 1840s, wine was being produced on the South Fork. In his book on viticulture and winemaking published in Brooklyn in 1846, Alden Spooner mentions that grapes were being grown for wine in Southampton. Winemaking persisted on Long Island up through the mid-twentieth century, due mainly to the efforts of amateurs.

As farmers of other nationalities followed the English, they brought their own vinous interests with them. The Italians, in particular, often made wine either from local grapes or from grapes shipped in from California by freight car. East End farmers, seeking to diversify their crops beyond the declining bulk staples of potatoes and cauliflower, experimented with alternative crops. One of those farmers, John Wickham, planted table grapes, including vinifera varieties, and played a key role in the rebirth of winemaking on the East End. There were also a small number of intellectual amateur winemakers scattered around the Island who made wine from their own grapes. An interesting example is R. Christian Anderson from the hamlet of Brookhaven.

With his long intelligent face, hollow cheeks and beard, "Andy" Anderson's appearance is strikingly Lincolnesque. In spirit, however, his affinity is clearly Jeffersonian. He holds a Ph.D. in Chemistry and in the mid-1950s was working at Brookhaven National Laboratory in Suffolk County. His notebooks of that period reflect their author's personality: rational, orderly, creative, humane and widely curious. The notebooks are very American in their confidence and openness to the world, but their broad scope is also very much of the eighteenth century. They could have been written at Monticello.

Some pages of the notebooks are alive with ideas for new experiments. There are notes on lectures given by visiting scientists; on a promising brain tumor therapy using beams of neutrons, for example. There are profuse diagrams of organic chemicals. The notebooks are not limited to scientific ideas, however. There are also architectural sketches of the modern house that the Andersons were planning, along with layouts for a home garden. At first these are simple vegetable plots, then more elaborate designs including orderly arrays of flowers, vegetables and a fruit orchard. Then, in 1953, following a discussion of the results of a chemical experiment at Brookhaven, there appear notes on the characteristics of various French-American grape varieties, and the garden designs start to include vineyards.

In 1954 Anderson planted two varieties of Seibel and one of Seyve-Villard. Soon his vineyard included close to 100 vines of five or six varieties. They were all French-American hybrid grapes, representative of a period of intensive hybridizing and experimentation that started in the 1880s in France. The stimulus in Europe for this work was the devastation of French vineyards wreaked by the phylloxera epidemic. In the United

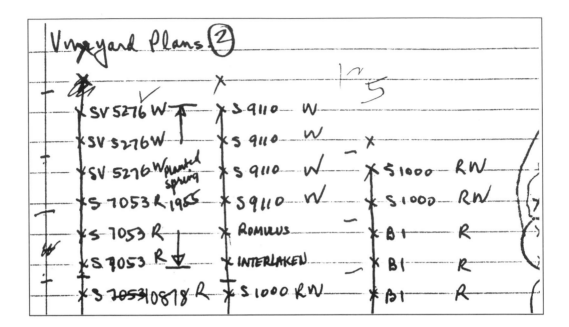

Detail from Anderson's notebook, 1953. (Courtesy R. Christian Anderson)

States such hybrids were seen as a solution to the vulnerability of pure European varieties to a wide range of American pests and diseases. With the chemical treatment methods available even by the 1950s, the pure French and German varieties were highly chancy in the damp climate of Long Island.

There was a second reason why Anderson chose the French American hybrids. In the 1950s there was little interest in, and even less knowledge of, Cabernet Sauvignon or Chardonnay. California was producing "Burgundies" and "Bordeaux" and insipid "Sauternes" which bore absolutely no resemblance to their namesakes. Seeking the grape varieties that had the best chance of producing good wine on Long Island, Anderson understandably focussed his attention on the hybrids. He pressed his first grapes in 1957.

By 1962, New York State had sufficient interest in the possibility of growing wine grapes on Long Island that they provided Anderson with a weather station to record climatological information to go along with his vinicultural experiments. During that time, Anderson endured one Job-like trial after another. His troubles ranged from bunch rot to hurricanes to flocks of voracious birds. His problems were not only caused by nature. Once, mislabled vines were sent to him by his upstate supplier.

Recently, Anderson understated his problems by saying, "We did have some edge effects." That is a laconic, scientific way of saying that his vineyard was so small that things happening at the outer rows of vines and at the ends of the rows had a large effect on the total grape population. As for the wine, Anderson confesses that, while it wasn't exactly bad, it was "completely undistinguished." Others have a much more favorable recollection of his wines, particularly the whites. Anderson eventually gave up his experiments, but they provided an important piece of evidence that quality wine could be produced from Long Island grapes.

John Wickham, although a teetotaler, has been referred to as the father figure of Long Island's wine industry. There is a certain Old Testament aura about him, and a quiet confidence that inspires trust. He carries his large frame and eighty some-odd years with evident strength and vigor. When you shake his large hand you can feel the texture of years of handling axes, shovels, innumerable varieties of trees and plants, rocks and quantities of good soil. It is said that he goes without socks in summer in order to toughen up his feet for the winter. Wickham's toughness, however, is more than skin deep. He is a traditionally religious man; the farm stand is closed on Sunday. One gets the feeling that his views, while expressed with courtesy and restraint, are strongly held and to be questioned at some unmentioned peril.

The rutted farm road to the Wickham house starts at the well known family farm stand on Route 25A in Cutchogue. The farm stand's reputation is based on the variety and high quality of the fruits and vegetables sold there, and the fact that all the produce is off the farm. No corn in May and no boxes stacked up from Florida and Israel. Wickham's family has been farming here for 330 years, and the Cutchogue Indians cultivated the land before them. The farmhouse dates back to 1659 and has been added to at various times in the style of the period.

Wickham became interested in growing table grapes to sell at his farm stand in the early 1950s. He wrote to the New York State Agricultural Experiment Station run by Cornell University in Geneva, New York, asking for recommendations. Cornell wrote back to say that there was not enough experience in New York State to form the basis of a recommendation, and they proposed a cooperative experiment. Wickham enthusiastically agreed, but said that he was particularly interested in the European, vinifera varieties. He eventually planted some 100 varieties of grapes, supplied by Cornell, about a third of which were vinifera.

At about the same time, R. Christian Anderson was starting his more modest experiments on wine grapes in Brookhaven, some twenty-five miles to the West. Wickham never met Anderson, but although he is too polite to come out and say it, he seems unimpressed by the chemist's accomplishments. Perhaps there is a touch of a farmer's condescension for the amateur vineyardist or a reflection of an unspoken rivalry. He is sure to this day that Anderson used the wrong spraying technique for his vines. "He used a high pressure sprayer, and should have known better," says Wickham, in a school-masterly way. "We always use an air blast sprayer, which gives you complete coverage."

Konstantin Frank, who propagated many of the vines supplied to both Wickham and Anderson, made several trips to Cutchogue during the course of Wickham's experiments.

The relationship between the gentlemanly, but strong willed men was not always easy. Frank, for example, was enthusiastic about a certain type of Muscat seeded table grape that was very popular in Europe. Wickham found that his farm stand customers didn't particularly like the flavor and, in any case, insisted on seedless grapes. When he heard that Wickham had torn out the Muscat vines, Dr. Frank was incensed and scolded, "It took 3,000 years to develop that grape and now you want it to be seedless!"

The beginnings of Long Island's modern wine industry can be said to date from a visit to Wickham's farm by Alex and Louisa Hargrave in November of 1972. The Hargraves had developed their joint interest in wine in the late 1960s while they were newly married students at Harvard, she an undergraduate in Chemistry, and he a graduate student in Chinese Studies. Wine was a natural accompaniment to food in their affluent backgrounds. Both Alex's father and an uncle were outside directors of the Taylor Wine Company. But it was in Cambridge that they fell under the influence of the likes of Julia Child and started to cook and taste French wines seriously. Gradually, they became more and more taken with the idea of growing premium grapes, and eventually making their own wine. The idea had an irresistible logic. They could continue to pursue their intellectual interests and their interest in wine, and at the same time do something more real, more tangible, than their business-oriented families.

A visit to the West coast in 1971 convinced Alex and Louisa of two things: that small, family-scale wineries making premium wines could be viable, and also that California was not necessarily the best place to make such wines. For one thing, land prices had already become uncomfortably high. When they returned to New York, the Hargraves sought the advice of John Tompkins, a Professor at Cornell, on where they could best grow vinifera grapes. True to the Cornell canon, Tompkins tried to persuade them to forget vinifera grapes, and to grow hybrids. But when he saw they were determined, he recommended that they visit John Wickham in Cutchogue. Tompkins realized that Wickham was not growing wine grapes, but that he had been successful in growing some Mediterranean varieties that were at least as sensitive to cold.

Before visiting Wickham, the Hargraves also gave some consideration to the Finger Lakes region where Konstantin Frank was growing vinifera grapes. After visiting his vineyard in Hammondsport, however, they concluded that despite his success with Riesling and Gewürztraminer, even he, the magician of vinifera, could not get Cabernet Sauvignon to ripen adequately in that part of the State. For the Hargraves, Cabernet was the measure of all things, and their next stop was Cutchogue.

Wickham was helpful and generous with his time, but did not encourage the young couple in their enthusiasm. He warned them of the risk of starting an entirely new type of agriculture in the area. Nonetheless, only a few months after that Thanksgiving visit to Wickham's farm, the Hargraves bought a sixty-six acre potato farm in Cutchogue. That same year they planted their first seventeen acres of vinifera vines, including, of course, Cabernet Sauvignon.

Wickham now seems quite proud of the fact that the Hargraves bought land "as close as possible to his farm, no more than a quarter mile away." Driving back home one night after dinner with the Hargraves, where the talk had been charged with Alex and Louisa's enthusiasm for their new venture, Wickham's wife said, "Why John, I think you're jealous of that young couple." Wickham replied, "I sure am. If I were twenty again I'd love to do something new and exciting like that."

John Wickham is not the only old time, God-fearing farmer in those parts. When the votes are tallied in national elections, Suffolk County is often one of the most solidly Republican in the country. Conservative rural values prevail; so also do conservative rural prejudices. The wine industry may be the saving grace of agriculture on the East End, but it sure is different from potato farming. What is more, the vineyard owners are not fifth generation farmers; they are advertising executives from New York City, or doctors from Connecticut, or Chinese Civilization scholars from Harvard, and there is the nagging suspicion that they are in it for the tax deduction or for some fancy winemaking make-believe.

Wickham agrees that there was a strong potential for resentment of the grape growing newcomers by the local farmers. It was fortunate that it was the Hargraves who came first, he says, particularly because of Louisa. From the beginning, she worked in the vineyards with their hired laborers, and put in longer days than anyone else. The locals, quite naturally, were curious, and somewhat apprehensive about the newcomers. They sensed that if one vineyard succeeded, others would follow, and there were differences of opinion whether that would be good or bad. When they got to know the Hargraves, however, and saw their dedication to their vines, and to the land that supported them, they were reassured. As others followed the Hargraves, there were many more stories of considerate, neighborly acts on the part of the local farmers than of conflict or resentment.

Legislation

It is not only the farmers and winemakers that have contributed to the success of Long Island's wine region. Legislators at both the state and local level have played a role in making that success possible. Governor Hugh Cary was a staunch supporter of the state's wine industry and encouraged the legislature to pass the 1976 Farm Winery Bill that provided tax incentives to small scale wineries. Subsequent bills allowed the wineries to hold tastings and to sell wine on Sundays. As it has turned out, sales from their tasting rooms have been extremely important for the financial viability of many Long Island wineries.

Suffolk County's Farmland Preservation Legislation has also played a crucial role in making vineyards a financially feasible option. Although the East End of Long Island has traditionally been a farming area, the value of land has increasingly been set by its value for houses and shops. Farmers have seen their taxes continually increase in response to that value. They have also come to realize that they could sell their farms, put the money in the bank, and receive a higher income for sitting in the Florida sun than for their current hard labors. That more farmers have not yielded to that tempta-tion is eloquent testimony to their devotion to a family tradition and way of life that, in many cases, is many generations old.

Soon after taking office as County Executive in 1972, John Klein identified the "per-petuation of farming and the consequent preservation of open space" as a priority of his administration. The vehicle that emerged to accomplish that objective was a program whereby the County would buy the development rights of farms and other open spaces. That is, the farmer would sell the right to convert the land to other than farming use for an amount equal to the difference between its value as a farm and its value on the open market. The enabling legislation was passed in 1974 and the first rights were acquired by the county in 1977.

That legislation has slowed the rate of conversion of farm land into shopping malls and housing developments. In a benefit never anticipated by its writers, it has also pro-moted an entirely new form of high value agriculture: the growing of wine grapes. By 1991, the price of farm land on the North Fork with development rights intact had come down somewhat due to general economic conditions. Nonetheless, an acre was still worth between $15,000-$17,000. At that price, growing grapes for sale to winemakers (at around $1,400 per ton) was clearly uneconomical. A better case could be made for growing grapes and making wine yourself, but even at that it would be extremely difficult to even break even. However, if the development rights were sold off, the land would cost about half as much ($8,000-$10,000 an acre) which makes it possible over time to make a profit. Not certain, mind you, just possible, assuming good luck, skill and a great deal of hard work.

Word Gets Around

The crucial secret of the atomic bomb near the end of the second world war was not any great formula, but rather the simple fact that the bomb was possible, that the laws of nature allowed a self-propagating nuclear reaction. Similarly, the modest explosion of wines that started to emerge from the Hargrave cellars in 1976, even with their variable quality, constituted proof that it could be done. Quality table wine could be produced on eastern Long Island from both red and white vinifera grapes.

Word started to get around, first locally, then around New York, aided by articles in the *New York Times* and the *New Yorker*. By 1980, three others, Lyle Greenfield at Bridgehampton, Herodotus Damianos at Pindar, and Peter and Patricia Lenz, had fol-lowed the Hargraves' path. Even earlier, David Mudd had established the first of what would be several independent vineyards growing vinifera grapes for the nascent Long Island wine industry. They, and others that followed, joined the Hargraves in writing a major chapter in the history of wine in America.

Selling the Wines

The successful development of a new wine region requires show as well as substance. It is not enough to make fine wines; the wine buying public must be aware that such wines are being produced and must be willing to buy them. A new wine region, like a new winery goes through three overlapping stages of development. The first few years are devoted to developing vineyards and to the maturation of the vines. Although wine can be made from three, or even two year old vines, it is only after five to seven years that the grapes have the structure and intensity required for wines of quality. The second stage is the development of the wines themselves: part experimentation, part patience. This stage adds another few years to a region's growth.

The third stage, marketing, is no less important than the first two, and no less time consuming. To many fledgling winemakers on Long Island, it has seemed to be the hardest part of all. The most obvious advantage of the region, its proximity to one of the largest and most sophisticated wine markets in the world, at times has seemed a disadvantage because of the infinite number of wines that are already available to the New York market. But that market beckons irresistibly to the Long Island producer, not only because of its size, but also because it can be served at low cost directly from the wineries, avoiding the twenty-five or thirty percent normally charged by distributors.

Long Island wines made inroads into the New York restaurant and wine store market (and from there to other parts of the world) first by the individual efforts of the savvy Alex Hargrave, and then through the knowledgeable efforts of Lyle Greenfield of Bridgehampton Winery and Bob Palmer of Palmer Vineyards, both of whom worked in the advertising field. By the mid-1980s, the region was starting to receive serious attention by the wine world.

In the summer of 1988, the first of a series of international wine symposia was produced by the Long Island winemakers. The Bordeaux Symposium, as it has come to be known, stressed strong similarities of climate between the East End of Long Island and the Bordeaux region. The symposium was held only fifteen years after the first vinifera wine grapes were planted on Long Island, no longer than a heartbeat on traditional viticultural time scales. Even so, some of Bordeaux's most knowledgeable viticulturists and most eminent winemakers attended. Paul Pontallier, the General Manager of Château Margaux, one of only four First Growths of the Médoc, was there, as was Mme. de Lencquesaing, the owner of Château Pichon-Longueville Comtesse de Lalande (usually referred to as Château Lalande) and her general manager. The United States was also well represented by winemakers from California, Connecticut, Pennsylvania, Rhode Island and Virginia. The symposium was reminiscent of the old saying, "Water separates the people of the world; wine unites them."

The technical topics discussed included the initiation of malolactic fermentation; chemical evolution of oak used in barrels, and its effects on flavors in wine; chemical properties of soils; and vine canopy management. Equally important were the many formal and informal occasions to sample Long Island wines, some of which use the same grapes prominent in Bordeaux: Cabernet Sauvignon, Cabernet Franc and Merlot.

The visitors were impressed. According to *Newsweek,* some of Long Island's Sauvignon Blancs were judged "better than anything in the Loire Valley." Château Margaux's Monsieur Pontallier was quoted as saying, "I like Long Island's Merlot better than California's because the bouquet is truer to form."

Surprisingly, Monsieur Pontallier also revealed a bit of envy for his Long Island confreres. In the principal wine areas of France strict laws (Appellation d'Origine Controllée) control virtually every aspect of winemaking: not only the particular plots of land and varieties of grapes that can be bottled under a specific label, but also how the vines must be fertilized and pruned, and the number of grapes that can be harvested per hectare. Pontallier said, "You know that we carry on a very old tradition with many important ancestors, and sometimes I have the desire to make vineyards, to plant vines in new areas like you are doing." So that no one would miss his point he added, "I feel very strongly about that."

The Bordeaux Symposium gave a shot-in-the-arm to Long Island winemaking. It added to the growing publicity given to the region and provided important technical information to a number of grape growers and winemakers. It bolstered the Long Islanders' collective confidence that they could make the big time, and it augmented their sense of community and coherence as a group of winemakers who were in the process of defining a significant new wine region. Fittingly enough, in that July of 1988, while the French visitors and their hosts and hostesses were listening to lectures, tramping through vineyards and generally comparing notes, the nearby grapes were quietly ripening into what would later be called "the vintage to put Long Island on the map."

Two years later, as those 1988 wines were beginning to appear from the winemakers' cellars, the group hosted another symposium, this time focussed on the emerging red wine grape for Long Island, Merlot. The 1990 Merlot Symposium attracted a plethora of industry leaders. Pomerol, for example, the Bordeaux region which has the world's most famous Merlot vineyards, was represented by Michel Rolland, owner and enologist at the renowned Château Le Bon Pasteur. The West Coast of the United States was also represented by some of its most prominent winemakers and wineries: Duckhorn Vineyards from Napa Valley, Clos du Bois Winery from Sonoma County, and Columbia Winery and The Hogue Cellars, both from Washington State.

Recent Long Island Vintages: 1985-1992

1992 Long and cool growing season and a wet summer with heavy rains in August, followed by a sunny but cool autumn and extended Indian Summer. Harvest began late with all the grapes barely picked by the end of October. A good size crop of healthy, ripe and flavorful fruit. Promises to be a fine to excellent vintage, especially for white grapes.

1991 Hot and dry growing season interrupted by Hurricane Bob in mid-August that caused some crop damage but provided some much needed rain. Modest yields of small but ripe berries of concentrated fruit. Harvest began early in September, at least three weeks earlier than in 1992. Excellent vintage.

1990 Hot and partially rainy growing season followed by a warm, dry autumn. Winter frost damage earlier in the year and ravages by migratory birds in summer substantially reduced crop yields but the remaining fruit resulted in a smaller than usual supply of balanced and elegant wines. A very good to excellent vintage.

1989 Unusually wet growing season. A number of sound and quite drinkable wines were produced lacking overall the extract and concentration of 1988, 1990 and 1991. A fair to good year of mostly pleasant wines, with a few above-average exceptions from producers who reduced yields and selected the fruit carefully.

1988 A long, warm, and relatively dry growing season resulted in very ripe fruit at harvest. The wines have deep color and extract and richness of flavor. An excellent to outstanding vintage.

1987 There was excessive rainfall well into autumn and the wines are generally thin. A poor to fair vintage.

1986 A hot and dry growing season resulting in concentrated and flavorful wines. Mostly a very good vintage.

1985 Hurricane Gloria ripped through the region in late September during harvest time resulting in a reduced number of average to below-average wines. Those vines that were unscathed made pleasant wines. A fair to good vintage.

Alain Querre, owner of Château Monbousquet in St. Emilion, cautioned the upstart winemakers of the New World. He quoted another French wine sage, "It takes two or three generations to create a new vineyard of quality in a vine growing area where they have never produced a wine of quality in the past," and added his own observation that judging from the history of the French regions and châteaux, "it takes more than a century to build the reputation of a vine-growing area such as Pomerol or St. Emilion."

Certainly, little can be done to accelerate the maturation of new vines, but the relevance of vine age varies between grape varieties, and between the kind of wines being produced. For some white grapes and lighter reds, acceptable wines can be made from four year old vines. Longer lived, complex wines made from Cabernet Sauvignon grapes are more dependent on older vines. Many of the Long Island vines have now achieved a mature age of seven to fifteen years. Seven wineries have been producing wine for at least five years.

But the ultimate proof of maturity is in the bottle. By 1990 Long Island Chardonnays had received national attention, and were providing embarrassment to their California counterparts in blind tastings. An International Merlot showcase, put on in connection with the Merlot Symposium, afforded an opportunity for a large audience to taste Merlots from eight Long Island wineries alongside similar wines from St. Emilion, Pomerol, the Napa Valley, Sonoma County and Washington State. The Long Island vineyards clearly demonstrated that, despite their youth (or their infancy in the eyes of Monsieur Querre) they were a force to be reckoned with in the world of Merlot. In fact, Alain Querre himself carried Merlots from Bidwell and Bedell Cellars back to France with him saying, "They're better than anything made in California."

Another major boost to acceptance of the Long Island region by the serious wine world came in the form of an article in *The Wine Spectator*. The November,1989 cover showed a white suited and red bow-tied Alan Barr in front of his Le Rêve Winery. The cover also declared that "Long Island has arrived."

Eighty different wines from nine Long Island wineries were rated in *The Wine Spectator* article. Thirteen of those were awarded scores of above eighty-eight on *The Wine Spectator's* one hundred point international scale. In the same issue a number of French wines, such as a Château Haut-Batailley, an Echézeaux and a Châteauneuf-du-Pape, scored in the low eighties. That issue reflected the interest of the *Spectator's* influential editor and publisher, Marvin Shanken, in Long Island wines and marked the beginning of the *Spectator's* regular coverage of the area.

The Wine Spectator appeals to serious wine mavens. Its recognition does not necessarily mean public acceptance. A more telling indication of the growth of the popularity of Long Island wines was a series of remarkable wine tasting parties held on Long Island and in New York. These affairs took the popular pulse of the industry, and at each occasion the industry was found to be healthier than even the winery owners realized.

In the spring of 1990 word spread about a benefit barbecue and barrel tasting of Long Island wines being organized by the Long Island Wine Council and *The Wine Spectator*. The party was to benefit Lyme Disease research at the University Hospital at Stony Brook. The driving forces behind the affair were Alex and Louisa Hargrave and Marvin Shanken. Alex had suffered seriously from an undiagnosed case of Lyme disease, and his vineyard would be the site of the party.

A strong theme of the party was to be the celebration not only of Long Island wines, but also the rich produce of the Island. The wineries would be there, and so would many of the Island's best chefs. The theme of the match between Long Island's produce, cuisine and wines would continue to run through the promotion of Long Island wines in the future. The wineries used the occasion of the first barrel tasting party to release their 1989 Merlots. The wines had not yet been bottled, but the invitees would be able to have the first tastes of these wines right from the barrel.

Party day was a clear and beautiful, with just enough breeze to temper the August sun. The Porsches, Jaguars and immaculately restored wooden station wagons in the rough field parking lot indicated that the Hamptons set had decided that this was the place to be. A line formed at the huge green and white striped tent, and the indefinable, but tell-tale buzz of a good party began to emerge.

Inside, a lively crowd, generally clad in studiously informal chic, were happily downing Long Island Chardonnays, Rieslings, Cabernets, Merlots and sparkling wines, accompanied by hors d'oeuvres made from local seafood, game and vegetables. Some 750 people later moved to long tables covered with red checked table cloths. Before the evening was over, and the bluegrass and zydeco bands played their last notes, an entire 280-pound swordfish had been devoured, along with 800 lobsters, 900 ears of local corn, 900 breasts of ducks from the South Fork, and eleven bushels of peaches from just down the road.

The organizers originally wondered whether enough people would be persuaded to pay $100 each to taste Long Island wines and local fare, albeit for a good cause. They had expected about 500 people to sign up for the barrel tasting. When acceptances passed that point, they stretched things and added another tent. They couldn't go beyond 900, however, and had to mail back over 100 checks.

Did the popular appeal of Long Island wines extend beyond the Island? The question was tested with another combined tasting with Long Island food, this time at a New York City wine and food mecca, Windows on the World, on May 7, 1991. When the Long Island Wine Council planned the event, they hoped to attract up to 500 people. It was a risk to commit to a ballroom at Windows on the World, but the restaurant had gone out on a limb many years before to put Long Island wines on their wine list. Spectacularly sited 106 floors above New York Harbor, the restaurant has a superb reputation, especially for its wine cellar and wine-related activities. The Wine Council hoped to add to the appeal of the New York City event by involving several of Long Island's best restaurants.

It was clear, as the early responses to the Wine Council's mailings and announcements came in, that the coming out party would be a success. The numbers climbed over 500 and a second room was added. As close to 1,000 checks came in, a commitment was made to take the entire banquet facilities of the restaurant. But the maximum capacity was 1,000, and requests for tickets kept pouring in. For the Wine Council's executive director, Phil Nugent, relief turned to frustration as he started sending back checks. Eventually, some 600 people were turned away.

The crowd was similar to the one at the barrel tasting the previous summer, but it seemed there were more serious wine tasters. The prominent wine and food reporters were there, as were the wine aficionados, swirling just without spilling, poking noses into glasses, gurgling, jotting down notes on tannins and hints of this or that flavor and even, to demonstrate their true worth, spitting wine into silvered buckets. There was also a generous mix of young professionals, some apparently ascending directly from their desks on Wall street 1,000 feet below via an elevator that only bothers to mark floors ten at a time. Hundreds came because they liked wine and were curious about Long Island's products. They had heard about them; some had tasted one or two. Some had the feeling that there was an important wine region emerging at their doorstep. Some wanted to understand what the fuss was about; others wanted to be up on the latest trend. Whatever the reason, it was clear that evening that Long Island wines were no longer a bright secret of Long Islanders. The cat was out of the bag.

The next summer the barrel tasting was repeated, this time at Bedell Cellars. By then underestimating the response to Long Island wines had become a tradition. They ordered even bigger tents and even more food. Over 1,200 people showed up, and almost 1,000 more had to be turned away. The zest for Long Island wines, or at least for parties thrown by Long Island wineries, was growing faster than fruit flies over a fermentation barrel.

Another indication of the area's growing reputation is that several wineries are now making private label wines for prominent restaurants on Long Island, and in New York City. Lenz Winery, for example, makes private label wines for the Gotham Bar and Grill and for the New York Restaurant Group, owners of Smith & Wolensky and La Cité. All of these establishments have reputations for the quality of the wines they serve.

For American wine regions, certain events stand out as watersheds in the wider, global perception of the worth of their wines. These are the rites of passage that attest to the maturity of a region in the eyes of the world. Such a watershed event occurred for Long Island wines in October, 1991 in the course of a four-day wine extravaganza in New York called the New York Wine Experience. Long Island's wines drew praise from such luminaries of the wine world as Corinne Mentzelopoulos, the owner of Château Margaux, and Christian Moueix, whose family is one of the owners of Château Pétrus.

The most telling event at the Wine Experience was a seminar/tasting in which eminent wine professionals were asked to identify various wines. One of the tasters was Jancis Robinson, a highly respected wine authority and writer. The *New York Times* reported that, after tasting an unidentified Chardonnay, she said, "I thought it was a Chassagne Montrachet," referring to one of the great white wines of Burgundy. "And I was sitting next to a British wine merchant with a very good palate. He thought the same thing." The wine turned out to be a 1989 Chardonnay from Gristina.

Traditional East End design in a modern winery building, Paumanok Vineyards.

The event was reminiscent of a famous blind tasting in Paris in 1976 when a Chardonnay from Château Montelena in the Napa Valley was judged best—by French wine experts—in a field that included four of Burgundy's most famous wines. The result caused a sensation in the wine world, as well as some embarrassment among the judges who had been vocal about their disdain for the American upstarts before the tasting.

Oregon takes special pride in its Pinot Noir wines, made from the grape that is the basis for the great red Burgundies. Oregon's vinous Bar Mitzvah occurred in the heart of Burgundy in a blind tasting organized by Robert Drouhin, a well known Burgundy negotiant. Although a French wine, a twenty-one year old Chambolle Musigny, won first place, an Eyrie Vineyards Pinot Noir came in second, ahead of some of Burgundy's most renowned wines. The result made a strong impression on Drouhin, who soon purchased land in Oregon and is now producing his own Pinot Noir there.

Some of the greatest names of French winemaking, including Rothschild, Moueix and Domaine Chandon are now making wine in California. The philosophy seems to be, "if you can't beat them roundly, then join them". The events at the New York Wine Experience raise the interesting question whether French winemakers will pay Long Island the ultimate compliment of buying or planting some vineyards and putting their name on a wine from Long Island.

Bottling machine, Gristina Vineyards.

CHAPTER 4

Vineyards & Wineries

*Wine is...constant proof that God loves us
and loves to see us happy.*
—Benjamin Franklin

The growth and nature of the Long Island wine region can only be understood if the motivations and objectives of the vineyard owners and winemakers are understood. In this chapter we provide brief descriptions of each winery and attempt to capture elements of their individuality. We have not attempted to describe or rate individual wines; vintages disappear from the market all too quickly. Each winery, however, has developed its own style, based on the tastes and technical approaches used by the principals. As much as possible, we use the winemakers' own words to describe what it is they aim for in their wines, and how they achieve those objectives.

Hargrave Vineyard

The origins of Hargrave Vineyard are the origins of modern winemaking on Long Island. The Vineyard is of far more than historic importance, however. Its wines are perennially some of the best in the region, and no less original and interesting than their makers.

It is not surprising that Alex and Louisa Hargrave make wines with integrity and character. The key requirements for such wines would seem to be a clear, personal vision of what the winemakers want to accomplish, and the knowledge and means to craft the wines to that concept. The vision must then adapt to experience, for only over time, as vines mature and as different techniques are essayed in the vineyard and cellar, does it become clear what works and what does not. When the vision is attuned to the feasible, fine wines can be produced; wines that express the fruit and the local terroir in a personal statement.

In this quest the Hargraves have several advantages. First, they have firm ideas about the wines they want to produce, ideas strongly influenced by French models. Second, they have been nurturing their vineyards for longer and have probably tried more experiments than anyone else in the region. Finally, with a shared vision and complementary skills, they work as a finely tuned team, sharing all of the myriad tasks of a vineyard from

Alex and Louisa Hargrave, Hargrave Vineyard.

planting vines to marketing their wines. There is an integrity and cohesion to their winemaking enterprise that few other vineyards can match.

Alex has a confident, commanding, scholarly presence. His slim tallness, some six feet and six inches worth, sometimes gives him the appearance of looking down from superior, patrician heights. He speaks with the colorful and confident eloquence of a stage actor who has carried with him off the stage bits and pieces of his stage characterizations. Even his walk has character, resulting from a back operation when he was twenty-two years old. It is the kind of walk that would be adopted by a brilliant actor to give a haughty individuality to a performance of Chekhov's Uncle Vanya.

Next to Alex, Louisa has a bookish look and a slight build, an appearance quickly dispelled when you see her hauling cases of wine around the tasting room, or pruning vines on a cold February day. Her wiry physical energy seems driven by an inner determination and commitment to her calling. Louisa has a completely natural warmth with people which balances a shy and bright intelligence. There is something old-fashioned about Louisa, in the sense of old New England virtues such as character, independence and integrity. A certain creative irreverence might be in Louisa's genes. Her grandfather was Norman Thomas: Presbyterian minister, editor of *The Nation*, prolific author, staunch pacifist, head of the United States Socialist Party, and candidate for President.

The vineyard is mostly Louisa's domain. It is she and her varying size crew of helpers who prune, hedge, spray and harvest as dictated by joint decisions with Alex. She is also the chemist of the operation, measuring the characteristics of the grapes as they mature on the vine and of the wine as it progresses though pressing, fermentation and aging. They have at times employed assistants in the cellar, and one, Dan Kleck (now at Palmer Vineyards) even attained the status of co-winemaker. It is Alex, however, who makes the critical winemaking decisions.

One day Louisa greeted visitors to the winery wearing jeans and a tee shirt bearing two crossed flags: the French and the American. In a way the Hargraves are deeply American. Both of them were raised in successful American business families and are products of the best private schools. Such an environment instills a confident instinct for success. Their second shared culture is France. The seeds of Alex's interest in France were sown one summer while he was still at Exeter. He stayed with a French farming family in the Dordogne region who made their own wine. That experience contributed to his confidence in the notion of a family-scale farm winery.

When Alex and Louisa started making wines on Long Island, they used conventional American, especially Californian, textbooks. They soon converted to French texts, however, particularly the great work of Emile Peynaud, *Connaissance et Travail du Vin*. It turned out that there was a happy congruence between the French wines that most appealed to them, and the wines naturally produced by the Long Island terroir.

Hargrave Vineyard's formal tasting room could be taken as representative of the whole enterprise. It is a room where individuality and personal creative taste win out over decorating rules. The east end of the room is dominated by a Tiffany stained glass window representing a farmer sowing seed. There is some elegant, antique furniture about with intricately inlaid wood and burled walnut surfaces. The Hargraves are the kind of people who have always lived naturally with antiques (simply calling them furniture) from this or that ancestor. These mostly come from Alex's grandfather's house. Next to the antiques are rough redwood benches of various ages and descriptions, probably from Sears Roebuck picnic tables. The effect is personal, classy, imaginative, idiosyncratic; all terms that could well be applied to the Hargraves' wine.

The winery produces a wide variety of wines, under various different labels. At the core are their classical varietals: Cabernet Sauvignon, Merlot, Cabernet Franc and Chardonnay which are sold under the cut-out lattice label. These are often some of the most refined versions of Long Island varietal wines. The Cabernet Sauvignon, for example clearly reflects Alex's immersion in the classic winemaking techniques of Bordeaux. The Hargraves can now afford to hold back some of their reds, both in the barrel and in the bottle. Late in 1992, one third of the Cabernet Sauvignon was still in the barrel.

More modest vinifera wines, often from younger vines, are bottled under the Petit Château label. There are also special bottlings using art photographs or paintings from Long Island museums for their labels. Some of these "lesser" wines warrant attention.

When Hurricane Bob almost destroyed the 1991 vintage of Pinot Noir, Alex made a Hurricane Bob Candlelight Burgundy that is a charming, light, silky wine. The Hargrave Pinot Blanc, made in fresh Italian style and called Pinot Bianco on the label, is an especially good buy.

Alex is informed on just about any subject relating to wine. One day over lunch the conversation danced gracefully over questions of the key importance of drainage of vine-yard soils ("the one thing that all of the Grand Cru vineyards in Bordeaux share"); clay soils, and why they seem to work in Pomerol and nowhere else ("an unusual geological condition, *mamelon argileux*, in Pomerol"); the competition for oxygen molecules between vine roots and the colloidal pull of clay; the French overemphasis on terroir; and the fact that the barnyard element in Chianti is not due to terroir, but rather to spoilage yeasts or bacteria.

This led to an extended discussion of yeasts. Traditionally in France, fermentation was started naturally by the yeasts that were present in the vineyard and on the skins of the grapes themselves. Gradually these wild yeasts are being replaced by specific com-mercial yeasts that are introduced, or inoculated, into the juice. When asked whether he ever made use of naturally occurring, wild yeasts, Alex replied, "Having a grab-bag of yeasts wouldn't make ours a modern wine," he said, " it would just take us back into the eighteenth century. We want something else. We produce wines from various grape varieties. They each need a different yeast. Is a single inoculant going to go great with Cabernet, Riesling, Pinot Noir? On the other hand, we conduct malolactic fermenta-tion, and we used to inoculate for it. We're now finding we don't need to; the bacteria are in the vineyard or in the cellar, or in the tank and they produce very acceptable mal-olactic fermentation. But I would never entrust my primary fermentation to a grab-bag of yeasts. I want to have the fermentation begin when the conductor waves his baton."

The image of Alex as a conductor is a fitting one. It conjures up a Fantasia-like scene: a deep cave, purple mists rising from a vat of grape juice, Alex wearing robes with cabalistic symbols raising his baton. At the first downbeat, every single yeast cell springs into frenzied, but coordinated balletic action to the rich sound of a full orchestra. The image recalls a comment once made by Louisa to explain their collaboration. "I am the science," she said, "but Alex is the magic."

For many winemakers, their craft would seem to be an accommodation of two forces: the pull of the idea of the wine they want to produce, and the push of what the local conditions, grapes and equipment can achieve. The Hargraves clearly have targets in mind, best represented by the complex and elegant wines of the great châteaux of Bordeaux. Paradoxically, to achieve their ideal, they feel they must interfere as little as possible with the natural processes that transform grapes into wine. Alex has defined his winemaking technique as "doing the least possible at the last possible moment."

The Hargraves call themselves non-interventionist winemakers. If that is so, how does one explain the chemical laboratory, the pumps, the computer controlled press and other stainless steel equipment that constitutes their arsenal of non-intervention. A hint to understanding this seeming contradiction is Alex's characterization of the stainless steel tank as "one of the greatest elements of modern winemaking in the last 2,000 years. The reason is that we can conduct cool, fresh fermentation and, without bacterial static, get a clearer, more resonant ringing of the fruit. We think that the closer you can bring your wine to ripe fruit the better your wine is going to be, now and into the future."

There are many paths that grapes can take on their way to their future, some of which will produce an acceptable product. Most will end in disaster (i.e. vinegar) and a tiny few of which will produce a product that will bring smiles of satisfaction to the likes of the Hargraves. Of the multitude of paths that grapes can follow, the Hargraves want to use modern technology to steer a very specific course, to complete malolactic fermentation, for example, so that by the end of fermentation there is no malic acid left for stray bacteria to work on. Louisa carries out her chemical analyses to be sure that the wine is on the right course.

Even so, they use the traditional oak barrels for aging their wine. The oak would seem to impart aromas and flavors that are quite different from their intended "flavors of ripe fruit," but for Alex, it's a matter of timing. "If we were making wine for the Presidential inaugural of 2040," he says, "we wouldn't put our wines in oak. There would be no need. Oak just accelerates the rate of maturation... but for drinking our own wine in our own lifetime we are left with this one great anachronism, the oak barrel." Thus far there is no alternative to oak in achieving the desired molecular complexity that comes with age.

Nowadays, the tannic taste of oak has become an expected component of the taste of expensive red wines. "Oak in America is like Snoopy's security blanket," says Alex. "It's what the public needs to taste in order to feel the wine has gotten the proper treatment." For the Hargraves this becomes a delicate balance. The flavors associated with oak are both expected and necessary in achieving complexity in a reasonable length of time. However, they are very careful in never letting the oak overwhelm the natural flavor of the fruit.

Hargrave Vineyards produces some 8,000-10,000 cases of wine a year, about average for Long Island. With their reputation, the Hargraves could certainly sell more. When we asked Alex about that, he responded characteristically by referring to a Chinese saying to the effect that the first stroke of a painting reveals the motives of the artist. It is a question of motivation. Talking with Alex and Louisa, one gets the strong impression that they have found what they sought in coming to Long Island. The fact that they have created an entirely new wine region seems almost incidental. For them, of more importance is the independent life they have created for themselves and their children. That life reflects traditions that they value, and it allows the creation of personal, complex wines in which, as Alex says, "the fruit rings true."

Hargrave Vineyard

Route 48
Cutchogue, N.Y. 11935
Phone (516) 734-5158
Fax: (516) 298-8565

VISITING:

Open: 11 a m – 5 p m, Daily, May – December.
Access for disabled provided

Format for Tastings: No Charge

Retail shop accepts Mastercard, Visa, American
Express. Picnic area provided.

Special Events: Guest Speakers conduct frequent wine seminars with comparative
tastings. Charge to cover the cost of foreign wines. Please call for schedule
of seminars and special events.

THE VINEYARD: 60 acres

Grape Varieties: Chardonnay (33.5%); Merlot, Cabernet Sauvignon, Cabernet Franc
(33.5%); Pinot Noir (16.5%); Sauvignon Blanc (8.25%); Pinot Bianco (8.25%).

THE WINES: Chardonnay, Pinot Bianco, Merlot, Cabernet Sauvignon, "Le Noirien."

PERSONNEL:

Owner: Long Island Vineyards, Inc.

Winemaker: Louisa Hargrave

Vineyard Manager: Mark Terry

Nuances of the terrain can mean big differences in sugar/acid content of the grapes.

GROWING AND HARVESTING

(left) Checking for spider mites. Ursula Massoud and Dan Kleck (right).

(below) Fred Frank hand-harvesting chardonnay grapes. Banfi Vineyards.

(inset) With each grape variety, there is an ideal balance between foliage and fruit. Gristina Vineyards.

(opposite) Dave Mudd's mechanical harvester rumbles through the merlot. Palmer Vineyards.

WINEMAKING

(opposite) Traditional ways — Fujiko Ryan checks sparkling wine for sediment. Pindar Vineyards.

(above left) Modern ways — Richard Olsen-Harbich assays a once or future vintage. Bridgehampton Winery.

(above right) Bob Henn weighs in a load of grapes. Pindar Vineyards.

(right) Oak and stainless steel in the winery. Hargrave Vineyard.

MARKETING

Presentation is part of wine's mystique. Jerry and Carol Gristina.

Chardonnay is a perennial bestseller. Hargrave Vineyard.

Winetasting events spread the word about Long Island wines — a good place to meet vintners such as the Hargraves: Alex, Louisa and their daughter, Anne.

Chacun á son goût. Tasting rooms at the wineries afford the chance to form your own opinion. Lenz Winery.

"...whatsoever a man soweth, that shall he also reap."
— Epistle of Paul to the Corinthians

Richard Olsen-Harbich and Lyle Greenfield, Bridgehampton Winery.

Bridgehampton Winery

Each Long Island winery has its unique personality. Some reflect the talents and idio-syncrasies of the owner. In others the winemaker puts his personal stamp on the wines, and on the winery's character. Some of the wineries that have been around a while have acquired personality traits reflecting their own successes and tribulations. In the case of Bridgehampton Winery, all three effects are apparent.

The dominant first impression of Bridgehampton is style, whether that impression is gained from its building, a sleek, clean, modern version of the Long Island potato barn, or from its artful labels which often use the work of *New Yorker* cover artist, Gretchen Dow Simpson. That impression is the creation of Lyle Greenfield, Bridgehampton's owner.

Lyle is a picture of creative energy. He often wears colorful, modish clothes, and his black hair miraculously stands upright in a two inch crew-cut. His engaging, pixie smile suggests that he is enjoying a clever, and probably ribald joke. When we met him we were not surprised to hear that he worked in the creative end of advertising.

Lyle remembers exactly when the vineyard bug bit him. It all started with a July, 1978, *New York Times Magazine* article about the Hargraves, who had recently released their first vintage. Lyle was strongly affected by a picture of the couple standing in the middle of their youthfully green vineyard. He went to visit the Hargraves from his summer cottage in nearby Amagansett soon after and was struck by the image of orderly rows of grape vines in the midst of potato fields. From the time of that visit, starting his own vineyard and winery became an obsession.

Lyle brought energy, enthusiasm and unusual creative gifts to the work of building a vineyard. It is interesting that in his description of the reasons for going into the business, visual images play key roles. But this is a tough business. It exists at the economic margin. To be successful, everything has to be right: the site, the financing, the selection and management of the vines, the wine making, the weather, the marketing, and the control of expenses. This generally means hard, unpaid work on the part of the owner. If only one element is missing, the whole enterprise is at risk. In Bridgehampton's case a poorly chosen site came very close to being its undoing.

In that summer of 1978, Lyle looked for land on both the North and South Forks. Price was the major consideration, but the property also had to feel right. Lyle finally found a seventy-four acre abandoned farm in Bridgehampton. He describes it as a strange piece of property, hidden from the road by a stretch of trees, and quite wild. To Lyle it looked like God's country. He bought the land in early 1979 and planted his first vines that Spring.

In those early years Lyle sought out help wherever he could get it. He particularly appreciated the telephonic council of Hermann Wiemer, the famed German-born winemaker of Bully Hill winery in the Finger Lakes region of upper New York State. In all likelihood, Lyle charmed his way into Wiemer's circle; Wiemer used to call him "the great winemaker from New York City."

One early Spring afternoon, Lyle was holding the fort in the tasting room when three young men came in, dressed in mesh shirts and greasy jeans. They looked as though they were more intent on pillage than sipping wine, but Lyle, friendly as ever, asked whether he could help them. They stated that they were looking for a deli. After giving them directions, Lyle asked them whether they would like to taste some wine. When they replied in the affirmative, he started with some basic distinctions, red versus white for example. Then with a quick smile, he asked them whether they would like to spit out their gum before tasting the wine. Lyle's approach was characteristically optimistic, good humored and humane.

Bridgehampton's sense of style is not limited to the outside of the bottle. It's true that their labels have found their way into the permanent collection of the Museum of Modern art. But their wines, based on what is inside the bottles, have found their way to restaurants in San Francisco and London and have been served at the American Embassy in Paris. The Bridgehampton style inside the bottle started to develop when Lyle Greenfield hired Richard Olsen-Harbich as his winemaker.

Richard is as laid back as Lyle is flamboyant. Lyle is clearly an indoor person; Richard has the aura of the outdoors about him, as a lumberman does, or a farmer. In fact, Richard traces his career back to an early love of plants and gardening. He earned his degree from Cornell in Pomology and Viticulture and got his first post-graduate practical training under Hermann Wiemer. He is not the only Long Island winemaker who entered the field from the viticultural or the grape growing side, nor is he the only one to point out the logic of that route. Grape quality is of overwhelming importance in the making of fine wine.

Richard Olsen-Harbich's approach to winemaking combines an appreciation of traditional European methods with a penchant for experimentation and risk-taking. In the European tradition (as passed on by Hermann Wiemer) Richard relies more on his own taste buds than scientific instruments for timing harvests and making wines. Unlike most of his colleagues, he uses warm fermentation and has no cooling jackets around his tanks. While most Long Island winemakers now take their Chardonnays through a complete malolactic fermentation, it was unheard of in 1985 when Richard first did it.

Richard is anything but a conservative and safe winemaker. He considers that in order to make great wines you have to take chances. "It's like painting," he says, "you have to take risks. some time you come out with an ugly result, but sometimes you come out with what you want." One example of his risk-taking is his use of indigenous yeasts. He used them, for example, after the wet harvest of 1989 when he was concerned that the water logged fruit wouldn't have enough flavor. In his view, the batches where he used the wild yeast had the most interesting flavors and elevated the wines. Richard considers that textbooks, in order to be safe under all circumstances, will often prescribe practices - high sulfur dosages and heavy filtrations, for example - that sacrifice quality and complexity. He is willing to skate on thinner ice to achieve more interesting results. "I like to look more at the Europeans and to see how they do it in practice," he says, "rather than follow [University of California at] Davis formulas. That's where my style comes from, traditional European practices, particularly Burgundian practices like long lees contact in the barrel and malolactic fermentation." Not surprisingly, this approach has led to some less than ideal wines, but it has also led to some brilliant successes such as the 1988 Grand Vineyard Selection Chardonnay, one of the finest Burgundian-style Chardonnays to be produced on Long Island to date.

For Richard, the issue of risk-taking in winemaking is larger than Bridgehampton. Conservative winemaking leads to uniformity and uninteresting wines, in his view, and he would hate to see everyone on Long Island turning out the same safe wines. Fortunately, Richard is not alone in these beliefs. There are other risk-takers among the winemakers on Long Island, but Richard Olsen-Harbich is one of the most devoted and successful practitioners.

One of the products of experimentation at Bridgehampton has been the gradual narrowing down of their line of wines. In the past Bridgehampton produced Rieslings,

Sauvignon Blancs, even a Pinot Noir and one year a rosé wine called Red Snapper. Those days are over. In most years they now produce two Chardonnays, the Estate Reserve and the Grand Vineyard Selection which are both vinified in the Burgundian style and aged in oak. The Grand Vineyard is made from the choicest, hand selected, grapes and sees only new French oak barrels. In addition to a Merlot and a Cabernet Sauvignon (both using North Fork grapes) Bridgehampton also produces a blended red wine called Red Reserve: Grand Vineyard Selection. This sophisticated and complex wine was originally a blend of Cabernet Sauvignon and Merlot, but Richard Olsen-Harbich is also a fan of Cabernet Franc, one of the rare red vinifera varieties that does well on the South Fork. Cabernet Franc will also be included in the Red Reserve.

The boldness and independence that characterized the beginnings of Bridgehampton also had their costs. Although Lyle Greenfield didn't realize it when he bought his abandoned farm in Bridgehampton, the South Fork suffers from a growing season that can be as much as four weeks shorter than on the North Fork. Even on the North Fork, the summer is barely long enough for some slowly maturing varieties such as Cabernet Sauvignon. In addition, by the late 1980s it had become clear that, even by South Fork norms, the Bridgehampton site was not favorable; drainage was poor and there were low areas that captured the cold air in the Spring and Fall. They tried everything they could think of, including a huge mechanical air circulator, but eventually, Lyle admitted defeat, sold off a major portion of the original farm and planted new vines a few miles to the North. The loss on the original site was said to be half a million dollars.

There is plenty of evidence from Bridgehampton's wines over the years that the South Fork can produce fine wines. There are two requirements, however. One is that the appropriate grape is planted, and Chardonnay is certainly one. The other is the very careful selection of the site, avoiding low lying, poorly drained locations. Gradually, those favorable locations are being identified on the South Fork. In 1990 and 1991, as the local newspapers were printing gloomy reports on the demise of Le Rêve and Lyle Greenfield's land sale, several new vineyards were being planted between Bridgehampton and Sag Harbor. Lyle, in a typically upbeat response to the doom-saying newspaper articles, expressed the view that "the experiment is really in its infancy on the South Fork."

Bridgehampton Winery

P.O. Box 979

Sag Harbor Turnpike

Bridgehampton, N.Y. 11932

Phone (516) 537-3155

Fax (516) 537-5440

BRIDGEHAMPTON

THE HAMPTONS · LONG ISLAND

CHARDONNAY
1988

A classic wine made from Chardonnay grapes grown on the
South Fork of Long Island. Crisp and delicate with moderate
tones of French oak, in Bridgehampton's acclaimed style.

Alcohol 12% by volume

PRODUCED AND BOTTLED BY THE BRIDGEHAMPTON WINERY
BRIDGEHAMPTON, NEW YORK. CONTAINS SULFITES.

VISITING:

Open: 11 AM – 6PM, Daily, May – October. Hourly tours include visiting the actual wine cellar. Access for disabled provided.

Format for tastings: No charge.

Retail shop accepts Mastercard, Visa, American Express. Picnic area provided.

Special events: Chardonnay Festival; July 4th Barbeque; Mostly Merlot Tasting. Please call for details.

THE VINEYARD: 10 acres

Grape Varieties: Chardonnay (100%).

THE WINES:

Estate Reserve Chardonnay, Grand Vineyard Chardonnay, Riesling, Cabernet Sauvignon, Merlot, Meritage Reserve, Hampton Blush.

PERSONNEL:

Owner: Lyle J. Greenfield

Vineyard Manager: Richard Olsen-Harbich

Winemaker: Richard Olsen-Harbich

Dr. Herodotus Damianos, Pindar Vineyards.

Pindar Vineyard

*"Pindar in the ninth Olympian Ode, having had his poems scoffingly
referred to by a senior and a rival as 'new wine,' says that he too had a
reverence for old wine but preferred his wine to be fresh like flowers."*

Alec Waugh, In Praise of Wine

Herodotus Damianos is a man of compact stature and vast energy whose vision and force
of personality have had a profound effect on Long Island winemaking. A physician as
well as the owner of Pindar Vineyards, Damianos has set Pindar on a path quite different
from its peers on the North Fork. The most noticeable difference is one of scale. Rather
than the twenty to fifty acres that are typical of other North Fork vineyards, Pindar now
has some 200 acres under cultivation, and aims for at least 400 as the near term target.
Rather than fifty visitors on a summer day, Pindar attracts 500. They produce some
50,000 cases of wine a year rather than the typical 5,000-15,000. Of course, all is relative; in California, where several wineries produce half a million cases a year, Pindar
Vineyards would be considered a middling boutique winery.

Some on the East End have been decidedly put off by the aggressive scale of Pindar
compared with the normal, discrete Long Island winery. They object to all those tourists
who on a Saturday afternoon pack three deep around the two-sided, forty-foot-long tasting bar, giving it the appearance of a popular East Village watering hole. There is something unseemly about the marketing push. Where is the old world winemaking
atmosphere? Pindar's detractors also take pleasure in looking down their noses at some
of Pindar's products, particularly at the four popular seasonal wines: Winter White,
Spring Splendor, Autumn Gold and Summer Blush. Spring Splendor even commits the
unpardonable sin of containing cranberry juice!

"The Doctor" (as his colleagues at Pindar call Damianos) has another view. When asked
what his favorite wines are, he doesn't hesitate in identifying Winter White along with his premium red wine, Mythology, as his greatest achievements. For someone whose prize winning
Chardonnay and Cabernet Sauvignon were served at a George Bush inaugural luncheon, this is
startling. Mythology is a blended, Bordeaux-style wine, and is considered by some to be
the finest red produced on Long Island. On the other hand, Winter White is a modest, inexpensive white; pleasant, but with little finesse or depth. To understand why Damianos seriously
identifies it as a great accomplishment is to understand the philosophy behind Pindar Vineyards.

From the beginning the long term objective was to produce the "finest wine in this part of the world," an objective unusual only in the confidence with which Damianos expresses it. But he had another ambition: to have a real impact on the Long Island wine industry and on the East End of Long Island itself. He speaks lovingly and protectively about that "beautiful and pristine part of the Island" and sees the wine industry as its savior. Prominent on the cover of the Pindar newsletter is the plea, "Help keep the North Fork Green...Serve Pindar wines!" To have that impact Pindar has to be of a certain size; Damianos has to be a big player.

There was another major barrier to overcome if Damianos was to achieve his vision. As he explains, when he started Pindar, Long Islanders drank Budweiser and Coke, not Bordeaux. The average per capita wine consumption on the Island was 1.2 gallons per year compared with about four in California. To wean Long Islanders from their bottles of Bud and to educate them about wine became a mission for Damianos. The best way to accomplish that mission was not with some dry complex red wine, but rather with likeable whites. Ergo Winter White and its pairing with Mythology as an expression of Damianos's whole philosophy.

Damianos takes his educational mission seriously. Even now, he spends time behind his tasting bar, coaxing beer drinkers to appreciate wine. When they are ready, "the Doctor" will graduate some of his students and at the right time, move them on to the college level experiences of Chardonnay and Merlot. Some even enter the graduate school level of sparkling wines and Mythology.

Damianos divides the development of Pindar into three phases. The first phase, starting with the first planting of vines in 1980, emphasized the production of popular wines such as Winter White that could be produced from young vines. In the second phase, during the mid-eighties, Damianos felt that his vines were mature enough to produce acceptable varietal wines, and Pindar started to make Cabernet Sauvignons, Merlots, Chardonnays, Rieslings and Gewürztraminers. The seasons of inexpensive starter wines expanded to four and the first trial sparkling wines were bottled. During this phase, Damianos also started to plant the Bordeaux varietals Pinot Meunier, Malbec and Petit Verdot, which he brought to Long Island from California.

In Phase Three, starting in 1987, the horizons continued to expand. Damianos, aiming at a superior Bordeaux-style blended red wine, realized that he needed expert advise and engaged Dimitri Tchelistcheff as a consultant. Son of the famed enologist and wine consultant, André Tchelistcheff, Dimitri had established his own reputation as an enologist through his work at Schramsberg Vineyard and Gallo in California, and as the technical director at a prominent vineyard in northern Mexico, Santo Tomàs. Tchelistcheff also helped the island of Maui in Hawaii to become a producer of fine wines. His experience was crucial in deciding what combination of the raw ungainly pressings in 1987 would eventually produce an elegant, refined red wine: the first Mythology. Eventually is a key word, however, for as the blended wine aged in barrels, there was some concern that it was not developing as expected. Then, according to Damianos, in late 1989, "Something miraculous happened. Suddenly, the elements came together into a wine of "delicacy, balance and elegance."

The formula for Mythology has evolved over the years, and Damianos has been unstinting in planting Bordeaux grape varieties that can contribute to the blend. The blending of the assemblage is an important annual ritual, still guided by Tchelistcheff. Originally, the predominant variety in the blend was Cabernet Sauvignon. More recently, Cabernet Franc has made up the largest fraction, with the next largest being Merlot, Cabernet Sauvignon, Petit Verdot and Malbec.

Another important event of 1987 for Pindar was the arrival of Bob Henn. The people who are making Long Island's wines have brought traditions and experience from virtually every corner of the winemaking world. Bob has contributed his fair share of vinicultural cosmopolitanism, and more than his fare share of experience in unusual wines. A native of Illinois, his first vineyard experience was in Michigan where he made cherry and apple wine as well as wine from Riesling and Chardonnay grapes. It was in Michigan that he first met Dimitri Tchelistcheff whom Bob Henn calls his "major mentor." Tchelistcheff would, some ten years later, introduce him to Damianos. There were some important and formative stops on the way, however.

Between 1980 and 1985, Bob was vineyard manager and winemaker at Tedeschi Vineyards on Maui, Hawaii where he made the popular dry Maui Blanc from pineapples. With guidance from Tchelistcheff, he also started to make a sparkling wine (from Carnelian grapes) that would be served at President Reagan's inaugural banquet in 1985. In the next couple of years Bob managed to work in Washington state, Germany and Portugal before becoming Pindar's fifth winemaker

Under Bob's direction, Pindar makes some nineteen different wines, an ambitious offering for a winery of its size. Although many Long Island wineries now make a simple inexpensive white wine (a quaffing wine, as they say) none is as serious about such wines as Pindar. The four white and pink, inexpensive seasonal *vins ordinaires* have become extremely popular. In an average year, for example, Pindar sells over 10,000 cases of the soft and fruity Winter White. The rose-colored Summer Blush is an unusual local product. It is produced from Suffolk Red, originally developed as a table grape by Cornell with the help of John Wickham on Long Island.

Between the simple and popular seasonal wines and Mythology are a soft and fruity Gamay Beaujolais, two fine examples of Long Island Chardonnays, a stainless steel fermented and a barrel fermented version, two Merlots, a Reserve and a non-reserve, and two Cabernet Sauvignons. Pindar's non-reserve reds often represent some of the best wine buys on the Island. Bob Henn and his team also produce sparkling wines, a flavorful Gewürztraminer, a Riesling with true varietal characteristics and even a Port made from the Cabernet Sauvignon grape. One might imagine that the challenge of making this number of wines would be overwhelming, but Bob thrives on it. He calls it "winemaker's heaven."

Some winemakers are reluctant to single out a favorite wine variety, but Bob does not hesitate to choose. The apples of his eye are his sparkling wines. He makes three, all using the traditional méthode champenoise style. The simplest and prettiest is a pink sparkler called Cuvée Blush. Then there is a classical blend of sixty percent Chardonnay and forty percent Pinot Noir, a brut Premier Cuvée whose depth results in part from a full thirty-six months on the lees. But Bob's pride and joy is his Cuvée Rare, an unusual, dry sparkling wine with deep and complex tones made entirely from Pinot Meunier grapes. This wine was first made in 1987 and Bob recalls with evident pleasure the characteristics of the grapes at harvest: 3.1 pH, 18 Brix and 0.9 acid, what he calls a perfect analysis for a sparkling wine, requiring no additions of sugar or acid. This has been the case in virtually every year since.

Pindar may have the most extensive plantings of Pinot Meunier in the United States. A close relative of Pinot Noir, the dark purple Pinot Meunier is a traditional grape of the Champagne region in France. (Dom Pérignon, however, avoided the grape in his first Champagnes.) It is now the most widely planted grape in the region. Virtually without exception, Pinot Meunier is combined with Chardonnay in making sparkling wines. A curious exception, and a distant predecessor of Pindar's Cuvée Rare, was a highly successful pure Pinot Meunier sparkling wine made in Surrey, England as early as the mid-eighteenth century.

The operations at Pindar, Long Island's largest winery, require the attentions of a sizable senior staff. However, it is clearly Dr. Damianos's vision that pervades the enterprise. It is, perhaps, the physician's sensibilities that account for Pindar's concern for its customers. This characteristic is clearly expressed in the broad spectrum of wines offered. It also emerges in the Pindar tours, which over the years have been the most thoughtful and informative on Long Island.

Pindar Vineyards

P.O. Box 332
Main Road
Peconic, N.Y. 11958
Phone (516) 734-6200
Fax (516) 734-6205

VISITING:

Open: 11 AM – 5 PM Daily. *Closed:* Christmas, New Years, Thanksgiving. Complimentary guided tours.

Format for tastings: No charge for most wines. $2.00 refundable charge for Cuvée Rare and Mythology.

Retail shop at winery. Also, Pindar Wine Store, Main St., Port Jefferson, N.Y. Mastercard, Visa, American Express accepted. Picnic area:, "Pavilion in the Vineyard," overlooking vines.

Special events: February, Cabernet & Kisses; March, Riesling & Soda Bread; May, Mother's Day; June, Father's Day; August, Lobster & Chardonnay; September, Pre-Harvest Jamboree; October, Harvest Festival; November, Champagne, Chopin & Caviar; December, Mulled Wine & Cornbread. Pindar also hosts a wide range of other events. Please call for details.

THE VINEYARD: 220 acres

Grape Varieties: Chardonnay (22.7%), Cabernet Sauvignon (20.4%), Merlot (18.1%), Pinot Meunier (11.8%), Cabernet Franc (11.3%), Riesling (4.5%), Gewürztraminer (3.6%), Malbec (1.8%), Petit Verdot (0.9%), Gamay (0.9%).

THE WINES:

Chardonnay, Reserve Chardonnay, Gewürztraminer, Johannisberg Riesling, L.I. Autumn Gold, L.I. Winter White, Spring Splendor, L.I. Summer Blush, Merlot, Reserve Merlot, Gamay, Cabernet Sauvignon, Reserve Cabernet Sauvignon, Premier Cuvée, Cuvée Rare, Mythology.

PERSONNEL:

Owner: Herodotus Damianos, M.D.
Winemaker: Robert Henn

Eric Fry, Lenz Winery.

Lenz Winery

Lenz is one of the oldest wineries on Long Island, and at the same time one of the newest. The winery was founded, and the vineyards planted, in 1978 by Patricia and Peter Lenz. An urbane and energetic couple, the Lenzs sold their very successful restaurant in Westhampton, The Moveable Feast, to start their winery. From the beginning, their approach to wine was as a companion to food. Along with Pinot Noir, their first twenty acres of vines included Gewürztraminer, which they perceived as the perfect complement to Southwestern American cuisine. Over the years, the Lenzs developed a series of well received wines, including two labels of Chardonnay, a Merlot, a Cabernet Sauvignon and a sparkling wine.

In the late 1980s the Lenzs' energies and attention were drawn elsewhere, and while good wines continued to be made, the vineyards started to suffer from neglect. In 1988 the winery was leased to Peter Carroll. Carroll and a minority partner, John Pancoast, also owned Dorset Farms, where they grew Chardonnay grapes. When Peter Carroll hired Eric Fry as winemaker early in 1989, and a new vineyard manager in 1990, Lenz winery was reborn, with a new outlook and an entirely new approach to its wines.

Despite Patricia and Peter Lenz's dynamic creativity, there was a dilettantism that pervaded the winery in their day. In contrast, while it may be a strange term to use to describe a winery, we would now call Lenz the most thoroughly intellectual on the Island. That tone starts with Peter Carroll, the new owner. Born in England and trained as an engineer, Peter is a management consultant during the week. It wasn't the romance of the wine business that attracted him, but the opportunity to run a profitable and interesting business.

Whether talking about the economics of the wine business, soil chemistry and physics or the French concept of terroir, Peter is always articulate, analytical and at times dazzling. On one typical occasion, Peter was sitting in the shade of an old maple in the vineyard courtyard, a Kirin beer in hand, and his three year old daughter in his lap. He spoke in perfectly composed paragraphs on the subject of terroir. The discourse ranged from the cynically skeptical ("the French concept of terroir may be nothing more than an obfuscation, a way of saying ,'only we can make good wine'"), to the imaginative ("an agglomeration of variables all constrained through cultural or other reasons to be within certain bounds may be definable. To use a statistical metaphor from factor or cluster analysis, there may be a domain of variables that defines a space in which we can make wine. In some sense you can call that space terroir").

When Peter Carroll was looking for someone to be the new Lenz winemaker, he wanted someone who had reasonably firm philosophies and opinions on wine. He also wanted someone who could "challenge the status quo and orthodoxy" that existed at Lenz. In Eric Fry he clearly found such a person, and someone with a compatible intellect.

Eric Fry is a fine example of the second generation of Long Island winemakers. In the mid-1970s courage was the primary requirement for someone coming to Long Island to make wines. Some would say you had to be nuts. By the mid 1980s, however, the region had developed a sufficient reputation to become a serious option for well trained, professional young winemakers, at least those with a spirit of adventure. Such a one is Eric Fry. Standing a good 6' 3" tall, with flowing reddish-gold hair, full beard and mustache, Eric cuts a heroic figure. Even in jeans and an old shirt he looks as though he stepped out of the role of a Verdi operatic tenor-hero. Even his approach to wine making has an operatic, romantic bent. Many winemakers on Long Island make wine in a Mozart, or even a Monteverdi style. Not Eric. For him, wines are romantic Puccini or gutsy Verdi. The barnyard earthiness of Burgundy attracts him more than the courtly elegance of Bordeaux.

Eric's development as a winemaker was influenced, in one way or another, by some of the greatest names in American winemaking. After earning his undergraduate degree in microbiology from the University of Indiana, Eric was headed for graduate work in genetics at the University of California at Davis when he was sidetracked by a job at the Robert Mondavi winery. Mondavi needed a microbiologist to work on the solution to a tricky problem of wine spoilage, caused by a wild yeast called *Brettanomyces*. He stayed on and was able to take courses at Davis to complement what he considers his true education at Mondavi.

Over the next few years Eric migrated between vineyards in Australia, Cognac and Bandol in Provence. He returned to California for a job at Jordan Estates in Sonoma County. In 1985, André Tchelistcheff, the renowned winemaking consultant, suggested that Eric apply for the job of winemaker at Vinifera Wine Cellars in upstate New York. He did, and became a successor in that job to Konstantin Frank, who is known as the father of vinifera wine culture in the East.

Not surprisingly, Eric's knowledge of the chemistry and biology of wine is impressive. The soils of Long Island tend to be highly acidic, a characteristic loved by potato farmers but not by grape growers. When asked one day why highly acidic soils tend to produce wines with low acidity, Eric gave an impressive summary of current thinking on chemical potentials across grape cell membranes. He also uses his understanding of the chemistry of sulfur in wines to achieve the benefits of sulfur with its minimum use.

But Eric is far from the coldly scientific winemaker. Quite to the contrary, he clearly feels strongly and deeply about his winemaking and his wines. While he is generally calm, controlled and carefully articulate, as he warms up to a discussion of grapes and winemaking he is apt to say things like "pH is incredibly important," "I agonize over acid balance" or "malic acid is my personal enemy." One day a visitor made the mistake of asking him which of his wines he was particularly interested in, or liked best. In the manner of someone who had been asked which of his children he wanted to sacrifice to the Gods, he shot back, "That's not a good question!"

When Eric first joined Lenz in 1989 he was thwarted from moving ahead with his own style of winemaking by what he has described as an uncooperative vineyard manager. The implications of that reserved characterization are that there were some knock-down, drag-out battles, and before long the vineyard manager was replaced by Sam McCullough. The choice, apparently, could not be better. Sam has much the same philosophy of grape growing and winemaking as Eric, who calls Sam a thinking vineyard manager. One of the most telling characteristics of the new Lenz is the strength and seeming stability of the classical winery triangle: owner/marketer, winemaker and vineyard manager. The fourth senior member of the Lenz team is Tom Morgan, the only remaining stalwart from the early days. Tom sits with Peter Carroll on the sharp point of the triangle, and is responsible for marketing and day-to-day management of the business. By 1990, that team was in place to create the new Lenz.

The differences between the old Lenz and the new was placed in sharp focus one afternoon at the winery when Eric brought out two bottles of Gewürztraminer for a comparative tasting. One was the 1987 White Label made by Peter Lenz, and the other was the 1989, Eric's first Gewürztraminer at Lenz. It would be hard to imagine two more different wines made from the same grape variety. Peter Lenz's wine was pale in color. It had a restrained bouquet and a pleasantly crisp, grassy taste with only a suggestion of the flowery, spicy Gewürztraminer character. Eric's wine, on the other hand, was much darker, almost a honey color, and had a huge bouquet of spicy floral aromas. Its flavor was typical of Alsatian Gewürztraminer, but its structure kept at bay any overt sweetness.

Eric explained that Peter Lenz and the previous vineyard manager, aiming at a crisp wine, picked the grapes early before the sugar content, as measured by degrees Brix, got too high. "Some people have the style to pick Gewürz at sixteen or seventeen Brix, because they're trying to protect the pH before it goes out of control," he said. "I don't pick Gewürz by acid or Brix or anything else. I go out and taste the grapes. When the grapes all taste like Gewürztraminer, it's time to pick, and not until. Forget pH. You have to have Gewürz flavor. Last year, for example, we picked at twenty-two Brix." This does mean that Eric often has to add acid in the course of making the wine.

Eric has made similarly dramatic changes in virtually the entire Lenz line. In common with a growing number of winemakers here and abroad, he has moved away from the big, oaky and exotic style of Chardonnays once so common in California and Australia. He aims instead, in the Gold Label Chardonnay at least, for a more Burgundian style of wine, one that emphasizes toasty and earthy flavors, rather than tropical fruit flavors; more "funky," as he puts it. This is achieved with barrel fermentation using a variety of yeast strains, extended contact with the lees and one hundred percent malolactic fermentation. The White Label Chardonnay, on the other hand, is lighter, more of a wine to have with food. Again, he avoids the clumsiness of some Chardonnays and accomplishes a balance of crisp apple, citrus and pear flavors.

Eric is rapidly increasing the production of sparkling wine, and has rebuilt a large cellar in the original Lenz barn for its production. Eric's red wines, the Cabernet Sauvignons and the Merlots, have a character quite different from those typical of the region where intense, fresh fruit flavors are the norm. Eric finds such wines too simplistic and aims for more complex, meaty wines that draw more on Burgundian winemaking techniques than on Bordeaux methods, even when the grapes are traditional Bordeaux varieties.

Like all winemakers, Eric is constrained by what the vineyards give him to work with. Lenz's vineyards have a variety of soil types and exposures, and an unusual range of plant densities: from 400-1,400 vines per acre. Batches from different vineyard sites are kept separate providing Eric with a rich palette from which to compose his wines. Even slight differences of exposure can result in batches with different colorations. For example, during the summer of 1991, nine months after fermentation, among the batches of 1990 Merlot in his cellar there were two that had come from the same vineyard and had been vinified in exactly the same way. The vineyard was on a gentle rise of land. One batch came from the part of the vineyard tilted slightly to the south and the other from the part tilted slightly to the north. As tasted out of the barrel, the two batches had decidedly different characteristics. The southern wine was darker, more intense and brooding, while the northern counterpart was altogether brighter and more accessible, but a trifle less concentrated. Eventually these would be blended in some proportions for the bottled wine.

Eric's style of wine making naturally leads him to age his wines, often in wood and then in bottle, for longer than is common in the region. His red wines in particular may not be ready for release two years after fermentation. The popularity of the current Lenz wines, ironically , is Eric's worst enemy in that regard, because as one vintage sells out, there is pressure to replace it by the next year's wine, whether it is ready or not. When Eric is successful in resisting such pressures, the visitor may find hiatuses in the availability of certain types of wine, but a specific request will often be fulfilled even when a wine is not offered for tasting.

Lenz Vineyard constitutes perhaps the most imaginative adaptation of local farm architecture to the needs of a winery. The architect, Mark Simon, clustered a group of farm buildings around a courtyard and further integrated the buildings through stylistic elements such as trellises, cupolas and a dusty rosé color. The visitor enters the courtyard through a narrowing tunnel in an ancillary building that enhances the feeling of entering a separate, magic place. The ensemble combines the honesty of old farm buildings, and the frivolity of the sparkling wine produced there.

Over the door to the tasting room, the visitor passes under a huge vine. Although not from the noble *Vitis vinifera* family, this riparia vine has its own reason for fame. *Vitis riparia* was one of the most successful native American species used as a root stock in the nineteenth century to save the French wine industry from destruction from the phylloxera epidemic. Without that intervention French wines might have evolved quite differently, and the Long Island wine industry, influenced as it is by France, may never have developed. So as you pass under this vine, give a thankful nod in its direction.

Lenz Winery

Main Road, Route 25

Peconic, N.Y. 11958

Phone (516) 734-6010

(800) 974-9899 (N.Y. Metro area only)

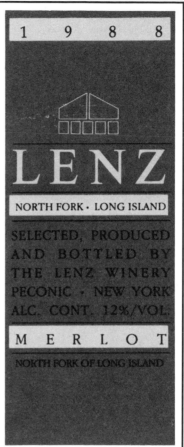

VISITING:

Open: Daily. 10 a m – 6 p m, May – Oct; 11 a m – 5 p m, Nov. – April. Access provided for disabled.

Tours: On the hour 12 Noon-5 pm.

Format for Tastings: No Charge.

Retail shop: accepts Mastercard, Visa, American Express. Picnic area provided.

Special Events: International Chardonnay Tasting, International Merlot Tasting, Guest Chef Food and Music Events. Please call for details.

THE VINEYARD: 60 acres

Grape Varieties: Gewürztraminer (15%), Chardonnay (40%), Merlot (20%), Cabernet Sauvignon (15%), Pinot Noir (5%),.Cabernet Franc (5%).

THE WINES:

White Label Chardonnay, Silver Label Chardonnay, Gold Label Chardonnay, Gewürztraminer, Blanc de Noir, Merlot, Cabernet Sauvignon, Méthode Champenoise Sparkling Wine.

PERSONNEL:

Owners: Peter and Deborah Carroll

Winemaker: Eric Fry

Vineyard Manager: Sam McCullough

Kip Bedell, Bedell Cellars.

Bedell Cellars

The worn gravel driveway that leads to the Bedell Cellars winery in Cutchogue skirts a traditional Long Island farmhouse, shaded by maples and close on to Route 25. The sign out front carries the Bedell black and white swan logo, but the farm looks much like the numerous potato-growing homesteads that dot the landscape of Eastern Long Island. It conjures up images of fresh vegetables and roadside stands, not of refined wines.

Across the driveway from the house is a sign with a painted silhouette, warning the driver that the farmyard kittens may be at play in the road ahead. The winery building is a barn reconstructed in a practical, businesslike manner. The one concession to the upscale is a pair of stained glass panels in the doors to the tasting room. A worn pick-up truck is parked outside, completing the overall impression of a small-scale farming operation that has changed little over the generations.

Only a few years ago, if you wanted to taste Bedell Cellars wines, you would knock on the back door of the sleepy farmhouse — most probably with a combination of expectation and tentativeness. You would then be unceremoniously ushered into the linoleum tiled kitchen for a sample. An unmarked bottle would be rescued from the elderly refrigerator, a couple of glasses poured, and the clean, delightful taste of Bedell Cellars Chardonnay would be revealed.

Today's visitor to the winery will get the same friendly, straightforward welcome. Inside the tasting room, long windows afford the visitor a view of the winery's equivalent of the farm kitchen: a combination office and laboratory with a jumble of technical books and journals, coffee cups, bottles (mostly open), test tubes and meters of various kinds, a small desk, a few miscellaneous chairs, file cabinets and, under some papers, an Apple computer.

An expression of interest on the part of visitors will give access to the inner sanctum of the Bedell winery. This large room at the rear of the building holds stacks of American and French oak casks, gleaming stainless steel tanks, hoses, and a variety of miscellaneous equipment. Suddenly, all the high-tech and traditional effort it takes to turn grapes into wine becomes apparent.

Kip Bedell started to make wine as a hobby in the basement of his West Hempstead home more than twenty years ago. First using concentrated grape juice, and then grapes from up-state New York, he would produce one to 200 gallons a year, and year-by-year, he would learn from the traditional teacher of winemaking: trial and error. An early lesson was that wine can only be as good as the grapes that go into it.

As he became more ambitious for his wines and increasingly more consumed by his hobby, Kip found it harder and harder to procure grapes of high enough quality. He started to muse over the possibility of a vineyard of his own. Familiar with the North Fork from childhood memories of summers spent with grandparents in Mattituck, Kip was naturally drawn to the then infant vineyard country on Long Island. He and his wife, Susan, bought fifty acres of land in Cutchogue that had been known as the Davids Farm for 200 years and planted his first seven acres of vines in 1980. Kip continued to plant over the next three years until nineteen acres that were once potato fields were covered with vinifera grape vines.

Kip is a quiet, thoughtful man whose apparently easy-going and laid-back manner belies a dedication and passion for the business of making fine wine. He describes himself as a self-taught vintner with only a modest bolstering by some courses in wine related chemistry in Pennsylvania. He continues to apply a persistent, intelligent trial and error approach to more and more sophisticated challenges of wine making.

Colleagues describe Kip Bedell as a workaholic (fine wine variety). As you talk with him about Bedell Cellars the impression that emerges is a combination of quiet pride, resolve and caution: pride in what has already been accomplished, a resolve to produce even better wine and the type of caution that develops naturally in a man who depends on the vagaries of nature for his success. In fact, it was only recently that he gave up the security of the family fuel oil business to throw his lot entirely with wine making.

Kip's natural caution must have been reinforced in 1985, the year of Bedell's first vintage. Bedell Vineyards had harvested its first fruit in 1983. The grapes were sold on the market that year and the next. By 1985 they were ready to produce their first vintage in what turned out to be a Bacchanalian trial by fire. The newly constructed winery's cement floors were being poured during the harvest so the must (newly crushed grapes) had to be fermented outdoors, the fermenting tanks located practically in the vineyard itself. Plans for a deliberate, careful harvest, were thrown aside when news came through that Hurricane Gloria, packing winds that would tear every bunch of grapes from its vine, was heading straight for the East End of Long Island. The Chardonnay harvest was accelerated and the storm roared through, destroying most of the red grapes and shutting down electricity for over a week. Wine making progressed outside, wet, haltingly and with borrowed generators and candles. So much for winemaker control.

In a typical understatement, Kip Bedell says of the attempt to make wine under those 1985 conditions, "we had a little more skin contact than desired" but admits it was the worst experience of his winemaking years. Quite naturally, he would just as soon forget the 1985 vintage, and he considers 1986 to be Bedell's first real vintage. In those first vintages Kip was advised by Gary Patzwald, who became the winemaker at Palmer Vineyards during its formative years.

Kip seems equally comfortable in jeans and workboots atop a tractor in the vineyard, in the winery laboratory, or buttoned down in suit and tie pouring samples and talking about his wine in the tasting room. One suspects, however, that he is happiest outside on that tractor, or in the wine room making wine. In the vineyard, Kip depends strongly on his vineyard manager, Dave Thompson, who previously worked at the nearby Ressler Vineyards.

Fortunately, when Kip is on his tractor the tasting room and office are well tended. On a visit you may well meet Bedell's marketing and promotion director, Cynthia Fuller. A nice complement to Kip's reserve, Cynthia is all bright-eyed and knowledgeable enthusiasm, not only for Bedell's wines, but for the region as a whole. She is an energetic and effective spokesperson.

Bedell Cellars has become one of Long Island's finest vineyard/wineries producing top-flight Chardonnay, Merlot, Cabernet Sauvignon, Gewürztraminer, Riesling and Cabernet Franc. Current annual production is some 6,000-7,000 cases, a figure which continues to rise as Bedell gradually expands on the thirty acres now under cultivation. For several years Bedell wines have been represented on some of the best dressed wine lists on Long Island and in New York City. Establishments offering their wine include the Union Square Cafe, an American Place, Smith and Wolensky and Windows on the World.

Kip Bedell's style of wine making has evolved over the years and reflects the direct honesty of his personality. It also reflects a respect for fine grapes evident in the search that led from his basement in West Hempstead to the vineyards of the North Fork. Fine wines should reveal the nature of the fruit from which they are made. Kip believes in coaxing the wines to simply and naturally make themselves with the minimum of tinkering by the winemaker. He handles and filters the wine as little as possible. This may sound easy, but when the objective is wines of subtlety and character, it is anything but.

Bedell Vineyards does not yet grow enough grapes to satisfy its wine production, requiring purchases from other local growers. Even for purchased fruit, however, Kip Bedell maintains some control. Growers are happy to farm their vines according to his specifications when they see his knowledge and purpose. This is an example of a spirit of cooperation and even camaraderie that overcomes a natural rivalry in the region. It derives from a feeling of common purpose that often characterizes new, entrepreneurial activities. It is not surprising, for example, to see a neighboring vintner pumping his wine into a borrowed Bedell tank for temporary cooling or to hear Kip praise another winemaker's style of Chardonnay.

In keeping with this cooperative spirit, Long Island winemakers get together occasionally as an informal group to discuss common problems and to taste each other's wines. Kip Bedell smiles when he recounts that not everyone in this group always identifies his own wine.

Only slowly are traditions of winemaking being established on Long Island. There are no rules or preconceptions to live up to or to break. Kip Bedell and the other winemakers are still experimenting and working to establish those traditions. A spirit of perseverance and innovation, coupled with an open mind, prevails at Bedell Cellars. Kip claims that this means that new technology is welcome and that he feels free to try varied and unorthodox approaches.

A good example of a creative, opportunistic approach to making wine is encountered in Bedell Cellars 1987 late harvest Chardonnay. A parcel of Chardonnay was attacked by the grape rot, botrytis, in the wet, late summer of 1987. Emulating the process that makes the great sweet wines of Sauterne and the Rhine, Kip decided to harvest the fruit anyway, just to see how a late-harvest, noble-rot infested Chardonnay would fare. The result was an intense and unctuous dessert wine that most wine buffs would be hard pressed to identify as Chardonnay.

Modern technology takes a lead role on the vineyard stage at picking time when Kip Bedell uses a mechanical harvester. This extraordinary machine gently coaxes the clusters from the vine, but must be handled carefully to avoid grape or trunk damage. While some producers claim that hand-picking yields superior fruit, Bedell finds in practice that there is little difference to compensate for the slowness and higher cost of hand picking. When grape rot is a problem at harvest time, Kip sends pickers through the vineyard to drop the unwanted fruit to the ground before the harvesting machine marches through.

At present, Bedell makes two different Chardonnays which together constitute one half of the winery's output. The Bedell Silver Label Chardonnay is tank fermented in stainless steel, yielding a full rich wine with a hint of the flavor of tropical fruit. For those who like big, oaky Chardonnays, Bedell also makes a barrel fermented reserve which is typically loaded with big, round, oaky, pineapple and fig flavors. Both Chardonnays mature in French Allier or Nevers oak barrels, approximately one third of which are new in any vintage. The Reserve Chardonnay usually completes its fermentation faster and at a higher temperature than the Silver Label, but seems to need a little more time in the bottle to reach its true potential.

Bedell produces two other white wines, Gewürztraminer and Riesling, in much smaller quantities. A less expensive, proprietary bottling called Cygnet is produced from a mixture of these grape varieties. The result is a soft, summer-style wine, ideal for sipping on the lawn or at the beach.

If Chardonnay is the main attraction at Bedell Cellars, Merlot is the rising red star. Together the two varietals constitute most of the winery's output. Macerating the wine on its skins for up to three weeks produces a well-extracted Merlot, with a big, briary, fruity nose. Bedell Merlots often exhibit some peppery spiciness and hints of Monterrey-style olive fruit that gives the wine additional intrigue. These wines are aged in French and American oak barrels, usually for twelve to fourteen months. Kip has experimented with oak from Minnesota, Missouri and Kentucky. A small percentage of Cabernet Sauvignon is usually blended into the Merlot for some added complexity and backbone.

Some Long Island winemakers eschew Cabernet Sauvignon completely in favor of Merlot because the latter requires a shorter growing season and is more predictable. Kip Bedell, however, remains steadfastly committed to his Cabernet wines. Perhaps Kip, under his cautious exterior, is a gambler at heart; willing to wait out the late ripening Cabernet, taking his chances with Long Island's fickle fall weather. In good years, such as 1988, the gamble pays off and Long Island proves that it is capable of producing classic Cabernet Sauvignon with deep concentrations of hearty cassis and cedar flavors.

Bedell Cellars' Cabernet Sauvignon has a greater proportion of Merlot blended into it than its Merlot has Cabernet. Maybe this is an example of Kip hedging his bets. At any rate, Bedell has approximately one-fifth of its total plantings devoted to Cabernet, and expects great wines to come from them. Kip says that the secret is curbing the vine's prolific growth habits by proper leaf canopy pruning and by proper site selection. Continuing the creative trail and error style of winemaking that has become typical of Kip Bedell, Cabernet Franc was planted in 1990 to test as a blending partner with the Merlot and Cabernet Sauvignon.

For the consumer, one of the problems with Bedell Cellars' wines is that demand exceeds supply. While Kip Bedell says this is the kind of problem he likes to have, it does mean that some of the wines tend to be released sooner than they should be. Particularly for the reds, we suggest that a few years in the cellar will reward the buyer.

Bedell Cellars

Route 25, Main Rd.
Cutchogue, N. Y. 11935
(516) 734-7537

VISITING:

Open: 11 a m – 5p m, Daily. Access
    provided for disabled.

Tours: Tours for groups of 10 or more can
    be arranged by calling ahead.

Format for tastings: No charge; Leisurely,
    informal, personal, educational.

Retail shop accepts all major cards. Picnic
    tables and mowed area near vines.

Special events or attractions: Yearly, call
    for specifics Mid-Bloom picnic in June. Barrel-Tasting weekend in August.

THE VINEYARD: 30 acres

Grape Varieties: Chardonnay (32%), Cabernet Sauvignon (20%), Merlot (35%),
    Gewürztraminer (7%), Riesling (6%).

THE WINES:

Cabernet Sauvignon, Chardonnay, Chardonnay Reserve, Merlot, Cabernet
    Sauvignon, Gewürztraminer, Cygnet (Proprietary White), Late Harvest Riesling.

PERSONNEL:

Owners: Kip and Susan Bedell
Vineyard and Plant Manager: Dave Thompson
Winemaker: Kip Bedell
Marketing and Promotion Manager: Cynthia Fuller
Tasting Room Manager: Susan Johnson

Dan Kleck and Robert Palmer, Palmer Vineyards.

Palmer Vineyards

Some would say that successful winemaking is mostly growing grapes, excellent grapes, and mastering the technology of turning those grapes to wine. What is often forgotten, however, is that no matter how good its product, a winery must know how to market its wines to be successful. Today's wine market is highly developed. Vineyard owners from all over the world hire marketers and advertisers to sell their wines on the world market, especially in the United States, where they can realize some of their highest prices. This is even more the case in the New York City area where there is the highest concentration of fine wine consumers in the country. Palmer Vineyards can compete in this world because it combines the expertise of a highly skilled winemaker, Dan Kleck, with the acumen of an experienced advertising executive, the winery owner, Robert Palmer.

Each vineyard owner on Long Island brings to the business a distinct set of experiences, talents and concerns. Bob Palmer's career in advertising has had a determinant effect on Palmer Vineyards. The winery gives the visitor the sense of a distinctive product, offered in a distinctive package. Also evident is the impression of confident professionalism, the same impression that is given by Bob Palmer himself. "From day one we set out to be the best winery on Long Island," he says, and he is not bashful in claiming to have achieved that objective.

Although Bob lived in Huntington for a number of years, his advertising career often took him to San Francisco, and in the 1960s he started visiting the California wine country. To this day, his benchmarks are the wines from Napa Valley. When pressed to name a more specific model, he cites Mondavi, a winery that for him represents consistent quality and value. In 1978, Bob sold his advertising agency to a French group. With the proceeds in his pocket he started to look for land on Long Island on which to grow grapes for sale to wineries. He then realized that in selling grapes, he could be just as dependent on a few large clients, and just as worried that he might lose one, as he had been in the advertising business. This concern led him into the wine business where he would have 10,000 customers rather than ten.

The Palmer vineyards were planted in 1983 by David Mudd. Bob produced some wine in 1985 for the wedding of his daughter, but the first official vintage was 1986 when their first Chardonnay and Merlot was produced for public consumption. Palmer now produces about 10,000 cases a year. When Bob is asked how big he wants the winery to be, his key word in addressing the question is "hands-on." He feels that wine must be hand crafted, and he believes that beyond a certain point, a vineyard loses the hands-on touch. If they made only a single wine, a Chardonnay, for example, that point might be 20,000 cases. However, Bob likes to make a variety of wines: Chardonnay, Merlot, Cabernet Franc, Cabernet Sauvignon, a sweet desert wine and a sparkling wine. Each requires special treatment, and with such variety he feels that the hands-on quality is lost beyond about 14,000 cases a year.

A lesson Bob brings from his advertising business is to "respect the intelligence of the consumer." As an example of this, he sites Palmer's House White Wine, produced particularly for restaurants, which he clearly distinguishes from his vinifera wines by placing it in larger bottles with a different style label. The wine usually contains no Long Island grapes, but is made mostly from Riesling and Ravat Blanc from upper New York State.

Bob's marketing flair is evident throughout the winery, from the conservative labels evocative of a Bordeaux château, to the tasting rooms which include artifacts from the Mason Arms and the Hotel Majestic, two Eighteenth Century British pubs. Bob's marketing skills, and the consistent quality of Palmer's vinifera wines, have earned the winery a place on wine lists in London and San Francisco as well as in Florida, North Carolina, Massachusetts and Connecticut. Palmer wines have recently been accepted by American Airlines for their first class service.

The style of a vineyard is as much the doing of the winemaker as the owner. But winemakers can change, and such a change can be confusing to wine lovers who look for consistency over time in a winery's product. In some cases, however, what is lost in consistency is more than made up for in the evolution of the wine. Palmer is a perfect case in point. It can be argued that a succession of two fine winemakers at Palmer has resulted in a product that would not have been produced by either one individually.

Gary Patzwald, Palmer's winemaker from 1986 to 1990, established a distinctively clean, almost austere style for Palmer wines. In his white wines, Gary aimed for fresh, tart, green apple flavors and, unique in the region, never used malolactic fermentation to soften his wines. His reds were typically unblended pure varietals. The flavors of all of his wines, many of which are still available, are as close as one can get to the pure flavors of the grape. The joke went around that Gary resigned and left the region (preferring that to *hari kari*) when some stray malolactic bacteria produced a secondary fermentation that softened a late harvest Riesling.

When Dan Kleck became Palmer's winemaker and manager in the summer of 1991, he was already a popular and important figure on the Long Island wine scene and had strongly held views on winemaking. One of the reasons for Dan's popularity and success is his enthusiasm for what he does. "It's a great job," he says, "I love it."

Dan has the solid, clean cut, athletic look of a high school football star, along with the easy confidence that is often the long term reward of early athletic prowess. He acquired his winemaking knowledge through apprenticeship, and from all the books he could lay his hands on. He was drawn to Long Island in 1979 after a stint with the Tabor Hills Vineyard in Michigan. Impressed by the wines being produced by the Hargraves, he applied to them for a job and was hired on as cellar master. Over time he earned the title of co-winemaker. From the Hargraves, he absorbed the Long Island-French connection, and he often characterizes wines that he likes as elegant or stylish.

By 1983, Dan felt that if he was to continue to learn and develop as a winemaker, he had to leave the fold of his mentors. He started on a four year stretch, working as a consultant to many of the new vineyards growing up in the region, including Bridgehampton, Peconic Bay and Lenz. He gradually spent more and more time with Bidwell Vineyards and, in 1989, signed on full time when the Bidwells gave him the scope he was seeking to create his own style of wines.

Dan was also one of the central organizers of the two symposia that brought winemakers from Bordeaux to Long Island. Those symposia underlined the similarities between the two regions and provided Long Island winemakers such as Dan the opportunity to learn from the makers of the wines that he took as his models. At the end of 1990, Dan stunned the community by leaving Bidwell because of a disagreement over salary. He took a job with a new winery in Chile, but was soon lured back by Bob Palmer.

Dan's winemaking approach is quite different from Gary Patzwald's, although the two winemakers have high regards for each other's wines. In particular, Dan speaks admiringly of the vibrancy and liveliness of Gary's wines, and his ability to capture the quality of the fruit. When he signed on at Palmer, Dan did not see his job as remaking Palmer's wines to his own winemaking image, but rather to take the best of what Gary had done and combine it with his own vision of the final product.

In contrast to Gary's austere style, Dan aims for darker, more complex, more highly developed flavors, and wines that are mature by the time of their release. He favors dry fruit, leathery flavors in some of his wines, which he achieves. He uses a partial malolactic fermentation for his white wines to introduce a buttery softness, while retaining some of the malic acid that is responsible for the fruity crispness. He generally produces two Chardonnays. One is on the crisp, fruity side, produced by fermentation in stainless steel tanks, with a minority of the mixture having undergone malolactic conversion. The other is a barrel fermented version with roughly seventy percent having undergone malolactic fermentation. This version is aged in new oak and has extended contact with the lees. It is a deeper, more complex wine, requiring more bottle age to show its stuff. In his Gewürztraminer, Dan retains a slight amount (0.5 percent) of residual sugar to soften the edge of what was, in Gary's version, a bone dry wine.

In his red wines Dan manipulates and aerates his wines considerably more than Gary did. He also blends significant amounts of other varieties into his varietals. His Cabernet Sauvignon and Cabernet Franc have significant quantities of Merlot, and his Merlot has significant quantities of Cabernet Sauvignon and Cabernet Franc. As with his whites, he aims for a somewhat softer and more complex wine.

Dan Kleck and Bob Palmer are giving increased attention to Cabernet Franc as a major red wine grape and are increasing their plantings of that variety. Another varietal being given increased attention at Palmer is Pinot Blanc, which they consider to be an important, more economical alternative to Chardonnay. A perennially popular wine at Palmer is their Select Harvest Riesling, a late harvest dessert wine with about five percent residual sugar. One of Dan's favorite varieties is Sauvignon Blanc, a wine that he introduced into the Palmer family. While most Long Island winemakers who make Sauvignon Blanc take the wines of Sancerre or Pouilly Fumé as their models, Dan takes the more unctuous wines of the Graves region of Bordeaux as his Sauvignon touchstones.

The replacement of one winemaker by another can be awkward for a winery and confusing for the consumer. At Palmer it has been neither. Instead, it has been a significant evolutionary step. Not only is Dan Kleck sensitive to the grape qualities that are characteristic of Palmer's vineyards, but he is also sensitive to the traditions of the winery and appreciative of Gary Patzwald's winemaking heritage. A highly evolved and sophisticated style is emerging at Palmer; a style determined on the inside of the bottle by Dan Kleck, and on the outside by Bob Palmer.

Palmer Vineyards

108 Sound Avenue
Riverhead, New York 11901
(516) 722-WINE

VISITING:

Open: 11 AM – 6 PM, Seven Days per
   week, All Year. Self-guided tours.
   Access for disabled provided.
Format for tastings: $.50/1 ounce taste,
   $.25 refund toward purchase.
Retail shop accepts Mastercard, Visa,
   American Express. Picnic area
   with deck overlooking vineyard,
   plus wooded picnic area in center
   of vineyards.

Special events: Fall Harvest Festival, every weekend in September and October:
   hay rides and live music. Voices on the Vine, poetry reading series bi-month-
   ly in July and August. Annual Yard Sale in June, discounts on certain wines.
   Please call for additional events.

THE VINEYARD: 50 acres

Grape Varieties: Chardonnay (34%), Gewürztraminer (16%), Pinot Blanc (6%),
   Riesling (4%), Cabernet Franc (20%), Cabernet Sauvignon(10%), Merlot (10%).

THE WINES:

Chardonnay, Barrel Fermented Chardonnay, WhiteRiesling (Select Harvest),
   Gewürztraminer (Winemaker's Reserve), Pinot Blanc, Pinot Noir Blanc,
   Blanc de Blanc (Sparkling Wine), Cabernet Franc (Proprietor's Reserve),
   Cabernet Sauvignon, Merlot.

PERSONNEL:

Owner: Robert Palmer
Vineyard Manager: Dan Kleck
Winemaker: Dan Kleck
Assistant Winemaker: Tom Drozd
Tasting Room Manager: Sue Skrezec

Jerry Gristina and Larry Perrine, Gristina Vineyards.

Gristina Vineyards

The situation of Gristina Vineyard's main building, which houses the winery and tasting room, is the first indication of the special character of this business. It is located well away from Route 25 in Cutchogue on the top of a rise that initiates a long, undulating plateau. The winery is as far away from the traffic as Gristina is from some its more market-oriented peers. Thus far, Gristina has managed to hold at bay modern financial pressures and to take the time necessary for the creation of fine wines.

While other wineries often try to make wine from three or even two year old vines, Gristina sold their grapes in those early years, making wine only in the fourth year. They were one of the first wineries to age their wines more than a few months in the bottle before releasing them. One of the last vineyards to pick their grapes by hand, they only begrudgingly moved to the era of the mechanical harvester. Their winemaking techniques tend also to be traditional. It all sounds a bit old fashioned, but in fact the enterprise is perfectly modern. The decisions are based simply on what will produce the best final product.

Gristina Vineyards engages the attention of three generations of the Gristina family, but it is Jerry Gristina, the co-owner with his wife Carol, who is clearly in charge. Jerry bears something of a resemblance to Dustin Hoffman, but an older Dustin Hoffman with greying hair, playing a mature and wise family doctor. Jerry is, in fact, a physician whose practice is in Westchester County.

There is a tremendous emphasis at Gristina on the vineyards. To Jerry Gristina, that is the heart of making fine wine, "It's effort in the field that counts. You've got to do it the right way in the vineyard." His enthusiasm tumbles out as he describes the steps they take to assure the finest possible grapes: confinement of the shoots by catch wires into a narrow, upright shape; severe hedging of the vines, pulling off leaves to bring sun to the grapes themselves. When Jerry was looking for a general manager and winemaker, he chose Larry Perrine whose experience was mostly growing grapes, not making wine. He chose his oldest son, Peter, to be the vineyard manager.

Peter Gristina has become a dedicated and astute viticulturist whose theoretical knowledge has been enriched through varied experiments in pruning and trellising. He possesses the patience and tenacity to cultivate the best grapes that the Gristina terrain can bring forth.

If it is Jerry Gristina who is responsible for the overall vision of Gristina Vineyards, and Peter who produces the necessary raw materials to accomplish that vision, it is Larry Perrine who has defined the vineyard's character through its wines. Jerry describes Larry as an artist who suffers, who worries about what he does. Indeed, with his graying beard, longish hair and worried eyes, Larry has something of a Dostoevskian look to him. A few minutes of discussion with him, however, makes it clear that Larry is a very practical artist who has thought through many of the issues and problems of Long Island winemaking.

This is not surprising, considering his background. A native of California, Larry earned his first wine pioneer stripes in Minnesota where he pruned the vines and helped make the state's first table wine. In the early eighties he demonstrated a practical streak in switching his graduate program from Soil Microbiology at the University of Minnesota to Enology and Viticulture at Cornell. While at Cornell he worked in the Finger Lakes wine industry and as an enologist for the State of New York, where he researched the growing of wine grapes on Long Island. He found himself spending a goodly amount of time on the Island, and became acquainted with Richard Olsen-

Harbich, the winemaker at Bridgehampton, Dan Kleck, then at Lenz, as well as other young Turks of Long Island winemaking.

When Larry was offered a job by David Mudd, the Island's most prominent vineyard developer and manager, he didn't hesitate to accept. That was in 1985. Soon thereafter, Cornell established a research position in wine grape research at their Riverhead station, and Larry was hired for the job. For three years he carried out research and addressed a range of practical vinicultural problems working along with the vineyard managers and winemakers. Larry joined Gristina two days before harvesting began in 1988.

Jerry Gristina's concept for the building to house his winery was to combine the functional style of the Long Island barn with clean, glass-walled modern design. The compatibility of these two styles is demonstrated in Gristina's combined winery and reception building, designed by Donald Denis of Aquebogue. The large reception room with its high beamed ceiling is given a touch of warmth by the couches and the rug in front of the large fireplace.

The glass windows and doors on the north wall of the reception room lead out to a deck which overlooks neatly tended rows of Cabernet Sauvignon vines. This particular field of grapes teaches an interesting lesson about the effects of small variations in growing conditions on the growth of vines and the quality of grapes. To the casual eye the field looks flat. Some woods at the far end, a mile away, declare an end to the vineyard. There are, however, gentle undulations in the field, a rise and fall of at most thirty inches over distances of 100 feet or so. These barely perceptible hills and valleys create mountainous variations in grape quality. In summer, once you notice the variations in terrain, you can detect a corresponding variation in the growth and color of the vines.

It is said that you can tell a lot about people by the company they keep. A visitor to the winery recently happened to glance into the small kitchen off the Gristina tasting room and saw a bottle of detergent, cups and saucers waiting to be washed, a few cans of soda , and two empty wine bottles. One of the bottles was a 1970 Château Latour and the other a 1966 Château Pétrus. Latour is one of only four great first growths of the Médoc, and 1970 was an excellent year. No better choice could be made to demonstrate a superbly balanced Bordeaux based on Cabernet Sauvignon grapes. Pétrus is the acknowledged king of Pomerol wines. It is so highly regarded, and produced in such small quantities, that it invariably commands the highest prices in all of Bordeaux. Château Pétrus is also unusual in that it is produced almost exclusively from Merlot grapes. Although the Pétrus vineyards contain five percent Cabernet Franc grapes, in two years out of three the wine is made entirely from Merlot, the most prevalent grape in the Gristina vineyards.

Those two bottles, drawn from Jerry Gristina's private cellar, are representative of the standards that Gristina, along with several other Long Island vineyards, are setting for themselves. They also reflect a quandary facing many Long Island winemakers. Producing varietal wines such as Cabernet Sauvignon, Chardonnay and Merlot reduces the opportunity to produce wines using an optimal mixture of grapes. In Bordeaux, Château Pétrus is a notable exception in that it is essentially based on a single grape variety. The wine of Château Latour generally contains Merlot, Cabernet Franc and Petit Verdot, as well as the major constituent, Cabernet Sauvignon. The particular mix each year is a function of the qualities of the different batches of grapes.

Not surprisingly, many Long Island winemakers don't like the limitations of a varietal wine, and Larry Perrine is no exception. He understands the dictates of the market place, but would like the freedom to find his own blend. He knows the areas where the grapes will come from for a vineyard designated wine. He also knows the ingredients: primarily Merlot and Cabernet Sauvignon, with some Cabernet Franc used as a blending element (Cabernet Franc was crushed at Gristina for the first time in 1991.) In that sense, of the two bottles in the kitchen, the real target is the Latour with all its polyphonic complexity, rather than the single voiced Pétrus, no matter how glorious that voice. Then again, we are sure Larry would not complain of a Pétrus, nor would Jerry Gristina.

Many vintners have clear conceptions of the wines they would like to produce. Those objectives are often based on wines they admire, such as the Latour or the Pétrus in Gristina's kitchen. Both Jerry and Peter Gristina expect the vineyard's reputation to be built on their red wines.

Larry Perrine's conception of the wines he is aiming at is shaped by the particular conditions of climate, soil and small scale geography he is dealing with. These factors present limitations, but on Long Island they also present tremendous opportunities, and the winemakers who will have the greatest success will be those who are the most sensitive to their particular terroir.

As a case in point, Larry points out the advantages that Long Island has in producing a Merlot, compared with California or the State of Washington. On the West Coast the intense sun and heat tend to ripen Merlot grapes relatively quickly, and when ripe, they must be picked lest the juice become overly concentrated and sweet. This is fine except that the tannins in the skin and pips are still immature. These green tannins tend to produce an astringency and an alcoholic aftertaste that is referred to as a "hot finish." On Long Island by the time the grapes ripen, the sun's intensity has diminished, and the grapes can be left on the vine to allow the tannins to mature. These fully ripened tannins, actually polyphenols, while still somewhat astringent, are less biting and produce depth and a mouth filling roundness to the wine.

These balanced, round qualities can already be tasted in Gristina's Merlots. They usually incorporate some Cabernet Sauvignon (ten to twenty percent) which adds structure to the Merlot's natural softness. Recent bottlings exhibit a dark, brooding quality that suggests they may evolve into true *vins de garde* — wines that will improve with considerable cellar age. As for all Long Island wineries, Gristina is aided by the fact that Merlot's attractiveness depends less on the age of the vines than does a wine from

Cabernet Sauvignon. The Gristina Cabernets incorporate some Merlot and show admirable balance and complexity for young wines made from relatively young vines.

From their first vintage, the 1988, Gristina's Chardonnays demonstrated complex citrus, melon and pear flavors and a fine balance, neither too sharp, nor too heavy. This is achieved by letting the fermented juice sit on the lees, a layer of fermentation detritus and yeasts, for several months. The wine also undergoes a complete malolactic transformation before aging in French oak barrels.

Jerry Gristina has his own version of the tug of war between the wines he most admires and what nature wants to produce on Long Island. For him the pinnacles of wine geography are the great red Burgundies, and he would love to produce wines from the noble Burgundian grape, Pinot Noir. This remains a troublesome and controversial grape on Long Island, in part because of its thin skin and greater susceptibility to any kind of fungal or physical damage. When Jerry started his vineyard, everyone told him Pinot Noir could not be grown successfully on Long Island. He took that as a challenge and set aside an acre to experiment with clonal varieties, the spacing of vines and vine management. He points out that the climatic conditions on Long Island are not that dissimilar from Burgundy, and no wetter than Oregon where some of the best Pinot Noirs in the United States are produced. One important innovation used by Gristina is putting the wire on which the fruiting cane is trained very low, only eighteen inches from the ground. To harvest the grapes, you have to lie on your back.

Jerry Gristina has an obvious enthusiasm for his vineyard and his own wines, but there is a deeper strand to his feeling. Once, when asked how he managed to combine the demands of his life as a doctor with those of running a winery, he pointed out, first of all, that it has been his income as a doctor, which he calls substantial, that has supported the vineyard. He then explained that with the current team and system in place — Larry Perrine as winemaker and his son, Peter, as vineyard manager — he no longer has to worry about the day-to-day operations. He referred to an event of a few years ago that he sees as a turning point in his relationship with the vineyard. He came out one Friday and was sitting down talking to Peter, who said to him, "Dad, we had a little problem during the week. A worker driving a tractor-sprayer took a corner too fast and the sprayer turned over and was a little damaged. I didn't want to bother you with it, so I had it fixed and everything is fine." Jerry thought of all the calls he did not receive that week. He told this story to illustrate why he no longer had to worry about the vineyard during the week, but what came through in the telling was his pride in the maturing of his son.

"In the beginning, before the staff was in place, the entire family was working very, very hard," he continued, "because we loved it. There was never an objective that said 'we must do this because we're going to fail if we don't, or we'll lose money if we don't do it.' The feeling was always, 'this is fun; we enjoy doing this. This weekend we accomplished this, and next weekend we're going to do that.' There was always something to strive for, together, and what greater stimulus can you have than working with your own family?"

"My father-in-law, Andy, who is 86 years of age, would come out with me since his wife died five or six years ago. I pick him up every Friday afternoon, and we drive out together; he stays with us over the weekend. We go out in the field and do the tough work, what we refer to in medicine as the scut work, the brush pulling, the worst jobs that there are in the vineyard. When I asked him why he enjoyed doing that he said, 'When we do it, then Peter doesn't have to do it.' That really gets to the point of what a family business can be like. If you've got the grandfather and the father working with the son, then it all succeeds. And that's why we named one of our fields Andy's field. It's the best of our four fields. One day we may come out with a reserve Cabernet, and it will be called Gristina Vineyards Cabernet Sauvignon - Andy's Field."

Jerry once described himself as a wine collector who let his hobby run amok. When asked whether he was glad he did, there was no hesitation to his answer. "Yes, and you know why? There is nothing more exciting than coming out and being told what to do by your own son and enjoying it." Then, looking out over his vineyards, he added a second reason. "This is the closest I'll ever get to being creative. There's very little that is creative in medicine, but we did this ourselves. We planted the vines, we pounded those posts and strung the trellising wire, and I did it with my three sons and my father-in-law. There aren't too many people in this world who can say they created something with three generations of a family. It's exciting."

Gristina Vineyards

Main Road, Route 25A
Cutchogue, New York 11935
(516) 734-7089

VISITING

Open: 11 AM – 5 PM, Seven
days per week. Please call
for winter hours. Access
for disabled provided.

Tours By appointment.

Format for tastings: No charge

Retail shop accepts Mastercard, Visa. Picnic area provided.

Special events: Wine growing Seminar, August; Harvest Crush Day, September;
Bud Break Renaissance, May; Barrel Tasting, June.

THE VINEYARD: 30 acres

Grape Varieties: Chardonnay (38.3%), Cabernet Sauvignon (28.3%), Merlot
(22%), Cabernet Franc (8%), Pinot Noir (1%).

THE WINES:

Chardonnay, Cabernet Sauvignon, Merlot, Pinot Noir, Vin Gris.

PERSONNEL:

Owners: Jerry and Carol Gristina

Vineyard Manager: Peter Gristina

Winemaker: Larry Perrine

Director of Sales and Marketing: Colleen Polye

Tasting Room: Steve Spodek

Mark Friszolowski, James, Kerry and Robert Bidwell, Bidwell Vineyards.

Bidwell Vineyards

In some Long Island wineries, such as Hargrave Vineyards and Bedell Cellars, the owners are also the winemakers. In these cases there is a continuity of taste and wine-making approach, which may evolve over time, but which creates a consistent and characteristic style of wine. In other wineries the winemaker is an employee of the owner, which creates a quite different situation. Each winemaker usually has a strong stylistic preference and in most cases has a determinant effect on the style of the winery's wines. If the winemaker leaves for one reason or another, there may be a change in style as a new winemaker puts his or her own stamp on things.

This is the case at Bidwell Vineyards. The first full time winemaker at Bidwell was Dan Kleck who previously had worked with the Hargraves. Dan became winemaker in 1989 after several years working with the winery as a consultant. At the end of 1990, however, a dispute caused Dan to leave Bidwell and Long Island. After a stint in Chile, Dan is back on Long Island at Palmer Vineyards.

Fortunately, there are three Bidwell sons, James, Kerry and Robert, who provide continuity to the winery's persona. They grew up with the winery, and they bring enthusiasm and specialized skills to the multiple tasks of running a substantial business. Bidwell Vineyards share with their North Fork colleagues the ambition to make first class wines from vinifera grapes, but from the beginning, they aimed at a larger output than most. While most of the other wineries at first aimed at a production of 2,000-3,000 cases, Bidwell produced 6,000 in their first vintage in 1986, and doubled that to 12,000 the next year. When Dan Kleck joined them in 1989, they were up to the current level of between 14,000-15,000 cases a year, small by California standards, but ambitious for Long Island. This meant that Bidwell could not depend on sales direct from the winery for any major fraction of their sales volume.

The scale of production has meant a significantly more active regional and national sales effort than is carried out by most other Long Island wineries, with the exception of Pindar Vineyards. The necessity of boosting sales has also kept the prices of Bidwell wines low. They are generally some of the best buys on the Island.

The Bidwell brothers manage the business side of the winery out of a shared, cramped office with assorted chairs and insufficient desk space. Somehow they also make room for their father, Bob Senior, the founder of the venture, when he is around. Walking from their helter skelter quarters into the winemaker's office/workroom is like walking from a nineteenth century London accounting office into a twentieth century Swiss laboratory. Jumble gives way to orderliness; second hand oak gives way to formica. The modest tasting room also contrasts with the spacious cellars and first class winemaking equipment. There is no question about the status of the winemaker at Bidwell.

During his years as consultant and then as winemaker, Dan Kleck created the Bidwell style. That effort started with careful attention to vineyard management, both on their own thirty acres and those of other growers from whom Bidwell purchased grapes. In creating Bidwell's wines, Dan Kleck aimed, in the French tradition, for a combination of elegance and depth. He was a strong advocate of malolactic fermentation for his Chardonnays. His style of Sauvignon Blanc was more in the soft spirit of Bordeaux than the crisp style of Pouilly Fumé or Sancerre. The formula seemed to work; Bidwell's Sauvignon Blanc is one of the most popular on Long Island, remarkably outselling even their Chardonnay.

Two aspects of Dan Kleck's departure from Bidwell were notable. First, it was considered to be important national news in the wine world. The most widely read wine magazine, *The Wine Spectator*, devoted a three column article to the news. Second, after considering winemakers from Europe and California, the Bidwells hired a winemaker whose training and experience was all obtained on Long Island. Mark Friszolowski, who grew up in Jamesport and trained on the job at Pindar Vineyards, can be considered the first of the truly indigenous second generation of Long Island winemakers.

It has become clear over the last few years that Mark has succeeded in filling the impressive shoes of Dan Kleck at Bidwell. Well over six feet tall, Mark has the military bearing and mustachioed mien of a Hussar cavalryman, combined with a youthfulness that is a reflection not only of his age, but also of his enthusiasm for his craft. Mark also has a deeper and more complex side that reflects an all too maturing combination of experiences: graduate work in English literature, some years in the Army, eventually as a second lieutenant, and an experience that puts all others into perspective, a serious battle with cancer.

The cancer was cured, but that brush with his own mortality left Mark dissatisfied with the Army as a career. He floundered for several months after leaving the Army, but when his father requested that he help with the 1986 grape harvest, Mark found his new calling. He applied for a job with Pindar Vineyards, where he soon became cellar master. Mark speaks glowingly of the dynamic, open, experimental, if somewhat authoritarian style of Dr. Damianos; the old school craftsmanship of the winemaker, John Jaffray, and the warmth of Pindar's famous consultant, Dimitri Tchelistcheff, who started his work with Pindar the same week as Mark.

Mark is very clear on some of the differences between his winemaking style and that of Dan Kleck. "Dan used to like to combine press fractions with free run fractions," he explains. "The free run is the first 110 gallons, say, from a ton of fermented grapes. The rest, requiring the exertion of the press, is the press fraction. At Pindar we would always keep the two fractions separate. It's three times as much work, but it's worth it." In other cases Mark has continued Dan's experiments, for example with different approaches and bacterial strains in malolactic fermentation of Merlot. Mark is unusually meticulous in keeping records of temperature at various locations in the fermenting vats, process times, pH and so forth. "I guess it's my military background," he says, "but a lot of people around here just don't keep records."

Mark's care is evident in his wines. A recently tasted Chardonnay was deep and savory, and the Riesling had a nice touch of tropical fruit. But it is with Sauvignon Blanc that this winery hits its stride. The 1990 bottling exhibits the varietal character of the grape without being too aggressive. It is a soft wine with attractive sage and mint flavors.

The Bidwell winery and office buildings reflect a serious, business-like approach, consistent with the scale of their operation. No reconverted potato barn here, but rather a concrete block structure attached to a commercial, aluminum clad building. A pale yellow paint job and a yellow and white awning over the entrance to the tasting room liven up the buildings, however. The tasting room is modestly scaled, but the visitor is warmly received and can taste Bidwell's recent wines in informative and pleasant surroundings.

Although the availability of wines will vary, depending on season and popularity, the relatively high production levels at Bidwell mean that a wide selection of wines are generally available for tasting and purchase. All will be worth trying, for all of Bidwell's wines are substantial.

Bidwell Vineyards

Route 48

Cutchogue, N.Y. 11932

Phone (516) 734-5200

Fax (516) 734-6763

VISITING:

Open: 11 a m – 5p m, Daily. Access for disabled provided.

Tours available.

Format for tastings: No charge

Retail shop: accepts Mastercard, Visa, American Express. Picnic area provided.

THE VINEYARD: 30 acres

Grape Varieties: Riesling (33%), Chardonnay (20%), SauvignonBlanc (19%), Cabernet Sauvignon (13%), Merlot(10%), Cabernet Franc (5%).

THE WINES:

Riesling, Chardonnay, Pinot Noir Blanc, Merlot. Future Releases: Méthode Champenoise Sparkling Wine.

PERSONNEL:

Owners: Robert and Patricia Bidwell

Winemaker: Mark Friszolowski

Alan Barr.

Le Rève/Southampton Winery

If there is a characteristic image of a Long Island winery it is the small, family oriented enterprise aimed at producing the highest possible quality wine. The vineyards and wineries seem to have grown naturally out of the agricultural tradition, particularly of the North Fork. Their architecture, often converted potato barns, reflects a parsimonious respect for that tradition. Almost universally, there is a strong emphasis on grape quality, which means growing their own, or buying grapes from neighbors whose growing practices are carefully monitored.

Le Rève's first vineyards were planted in 1981 in Peconic, on the North Fork overlooking the bay. They produced their first wine in 1986, but not until 1987 did Le Rève burst onto the Long Island wine scene with the opening of its grandiose, Norman style, copper roofed, brick building in Water Mill. Owner Alan Barr knew that the best grapes were grown on the North Fork, and he had fifty acres or so of vines there, but he also knew that the tourists were on the South Fork. One is reminded of Willy Sutton's answer to the question of why he robbed banks: "Because that's where the money is." The logic is irrefutable. The winery was said to cost seventeen million dollars.

It was not long after the official opening of the winery that rumors about financial difficulties began to circulate. The rumors were fanned by a community that regarded Alan Barr as an outsider. In an article in *The Wine Spectator*, Thomas Matthews noted that "Some members of the low key, close-knit Long Island wine community objected to Barr's use of off-island grapes and the ostentation of his winery." The term close-knit might indicate effect more than cause. Another winery owner observed at the time that the only thing that brought the heterogeneous, competitive owners together was their feeling about Alan Barr.

Barclays Bank held the first mortgage on the winery in the form of a demand note and, in 1989 informed Barr that they were foreclosing on the $6.6 million note. The foreclosure proceedings dragged on for almost two years, but were thwarted by Le Rêve filing for Chapter Eleven bankruptcy in January, 1991.

By late 1991, Alan Barr seemed weary and overwhelmed (he had also been through a bitter divorce and custody battle in the previous year). "It's exhausting being in Chapter Eleven," he said, "the public humiliation was endless." The Alan Barr of 1991 was a jarring contrast with the Alan Barr who had appeared on the cover of *The Wine Spectator* of November 30, 1988: jaunty and confident in his white suit and red bow tie, holding a glass of Chardonnay and standing on an acre of perfect lawn stretching back to his red brick, Norman winery. The cover stated that "Long Island has arrived," but the picture declared that it was Alan Barr who had arrived.

If Alan was weary of the fray in 1991, he was also defiant. He called himself a very tough street fighter and recalled his boyhood days in Harlem and Brooklyn. He said that he could not understand Barclays' actions. He was given thirty days to repay seven million dollars on a note on which he had never missed an interest payment. He thought there was an understanding that the note would be for five years, a claim disputed by Barclays. In any case, five years is a relatively short period of time for a winery of Le Rêve's scale to become profitable.

When Le Rêve came up in conversation during the late 1980s, the discussion would revolve around the personality of Alan Barr, the winery's architecture, the pros and cons of importing grapes from off the Island or, more and more, the winery's financial problems. What was often lost in the gossip was the fact that Le Rêve had been making some very good wines. In particular, the Chardonnays and Merlots made by Robert Bethel, Le Rêve's winemaker in 1986 and 1987, were as good as any made on Long Island. The 1987 Merlot was judged the best wine produced in New York State at the 1989 New York State Wine and Food Classic (the Governor's Cup). Le Rêve wines were also served at the White House. Ironically, the best Le Rêve wines of the period were generally not the controversial American Series, but rather the less expensive wines using exclusively Long Island grapes. Three of the nine wines especially recommended in the 1988 *Wine Spectator* issue were from Le Rêve.

With the disruptions due to Le Rêve's financial problems, no wine was made in the 1989 or 1990 vintages. When Russell Hearn arrived at the winery in 1990 as the new winemaker, the 1988 wines were still in the barrel. He did what he could to produce acceptable, saleable wines.

A central issue regarding Le Rêve's wines concerns the difference between grapes grown on the North and South Forks. Historically, Le Rêve purchased the majority of its fruit. In 1991, Russell Hearn's first full year as winemaker, only about one third of Le Rêve's 100 acres were bearing fruit. The controversial practice of purchasing vinifera grapes from off-Island had been suspended, at least temporarily. In 1991, the winery bought Chardonnay grapes from three growers, two on the South Fork and one on the North. In the Spring of 1992, Russell drew samples of each from the barrel for a comparative tasting. The South Fork grapes had experienced a more gentle and a longer life. While they started life some two weeks later in the Spring than their northern counterparts, they ripened more slowly under a cooler fall sun and were not picked until October 12, a full month after the northern grapes. The differences were striking, but they were differences of nuance, not of quality. While the North Fork wine had a more mature complexity, the Southerner had a fruitier, varietal flavor. One of the South Fork wines had been put through a malolactic fermentation and, surprisingly, had a decidedly more aggressive and brooding character. These were the promising elements from which Russell would compose the 1991 Le Rêve Chardonnay.

The antagonisms and controversy surrounding Le Rêve are fading into the past, and it is time to appreciate its qualities and contributions. The winery in Water Mill may be different from the prevailing Long Island vineyard style, some would say incongruous, but it is a consequential and impressive building. In winemaking, the inside counts more than the outside in any case, and inside the building is not only a magnificent tasting room, but more importantly, some of the best winemaking equipment on Long Island. The feisty Alan Barr has added spice to the history of the Long Island wine region, and the region is richer and more interesting because of it.

As this book goes to press, Barr's bankruptcy bid has fallen through, Russell Hearn has left to work for Pellegrini Vineyards, and the current owner of Le Rêve, Barclays Bank, has changed the name to Southampton Winery. This new venture will be watched with keen interest.

Southampton Winery

62 Montauk Highway

P.O. Box 962

Water Mill, N.Y. 11976

Phone (516) 726-7555

Fax (516) 726-4395

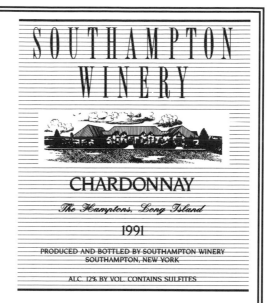

VISITING:

Open: 10 AM – 5 PM, Mon. – Thurs.;
10 AM – 6 PM, Fri. – Sat.;
12 AM – 6 PM, Sun.

Format for Tastings: No Charge.

Retail shop accepts Mastercard, Visa, American Express. Picnic area on patio with table and chairs, overlooking vineyard.

Special Events: Please call for details.

THE VINEYARD: 86 acres

Grape Varieties: Chardonnay, Sauvignon Blanc, Merlot, Cabernet Franc, Pinot Noir.

THE WINES:

Chardonnay, Chardonnay North Fork, White Riesling, Blanc de Noir, Merlot, Pinot Noir.

PERSONNEL:

Owner: Barclays Bank, NA

Winemaker: George Sulick

General Manager: Matthew Gillies

Sales And Marketing: Ted Kolakowski

Tasting Room Manager: Frances de Le Barre

Charles and Ursula Massoud, Paumanok Vineyards.

Paumanok Vineyards

In a way, Paumanok Vineyards is the epitome of the Long Island wine industry. It has both youth and age; innovation and tradition. One of the newest wineries on the North Fork, it embodies the owners' youthful enthusiasm for a life close to the earth, a lifestyle as old as civilization. Paumanok is the local Indian name for Long Island. In the choice of that name for their vineyard, and the care that they have taken to preserve the original barn buildings, the owners, Charles and Ursula Massoud, have shown their respect for the site's agricultural history. In the cellar of the restored barn are the traditional French oak barrels for aging wine, as well as the most modern, stainless steel, winemaking equipment.

The Massouds brought to Long Island not only their enthusiastic dreams of an independent rural existence, but also long family traditions in which grapes and wine were an integral element of civilized life. Ursula, warm and outgoing, recalls happy days of her childhood in southern Germany, working in her grandparents' vineyards. Charles wears serious looking glasses and has the demeanor of a careful scientist. When he and Ursula started Paumanok, he worked for IBM. He took early retirement from the company in the summer of 1992 to devote his full energies to Paumanok. Whenever discussions turn to vineyards and wines, relaxed smiles melt Charles' serious mien.

Charles Massoud grew up in Lebanon in its halcyon days and fondly recalls the sunny fragrance of his family's orchards. He learned to make wine in the most improbable location: Kuwait. The Massouds worked in Kuwait in the early 1970s. Wine was, of course, a necessity of life; a necessity which, in that strictly dry country, forced Charles to be his own winemaker. Grapes from Iraq were available in the local market, the *souk*. The Massouds crushed them literally by hand, and with sugar, yeast and informal guidance by other wine amateurs of the expatriate community, they eventually made a passable wine.

The Massouds came to the United States in 1978, hoping to make enough money to return to Lebanon to start a silkworm farm. However, in 1980 they read an article in the *New York Times* about the Hargraves and their vineyards. Charles traveled to Cutchogue to talk with Alex Hargrave and was so excited by what he saw and heard that he did not sleep at all that night. From that point on, the silkworms did not have a chance. Grapes and wine had permanently displaced them in the Massouds' dreams. Their restlessness was to recur for three years until, in 1983, they bought a farm in Aquebogue and, with help from Ray Blum of Peconic Bay Vineyards, planted their first 14,000 grapevines. The hard work had begun.

Charles chose to plant his vines in a dramatically different pattern than is the norm on Long Island. Instead of the usual grid of vines eight feet apart in nine foot rows, Charles planted his vines a mere four feet apart, thereby increasing the number of vines per acre from about 660 to about 1,100. His vines are trained to a single trunk rather than the usual two. In this he follows a common European tradition (and the approach used in the Mondavi-Rothschild Opus One vineyard in California) rather than a style recommended by the Cornell Agricultural Station for Long Island. With the single trunk system each grape cluster is fed by a larger root system, and Charles feels that it will make a substantial difference, particularly in his Cabernet Sauvignon wines.

Paumanok released its first wine, a 1989 Chardonnay, in the Spring of 1991. The wine had been vinified at Bridgehampton Vineyards under Richard Olsen-Harbich's direction and was a clean, understated wine that was an extremely promising debut for the winery. The Massouds' own Allier oak barrels arrived just in time for the 1990 harvest and by the winter of 1991, with the help of Russell Hearn, those barrels contained the vineyard's Cabernet Sauvignon, Merlot and Cabernet Franc. The latter was destined to be a blending component for the other, primary reds. When tasted from the barrel in the Spring of 1991, however, the Cabernet Sauvignon and Merlot were of such quality that the addition of the Cabernet Franc served only to dilute the vibrancy of the mixes. By early 1991, a fragrant, dry Riesling was also aging in stainless steel.

In 1992, Paumanok released a highly successful Burgundian-style Chardonnay. The wine is made from grapes drawn from two separate vineyard parcels, giving it enticing hazelnut and lemon flavors. In that year the Massouds also started to produce a refreshingly crisp wine from Chenin Blanc, a grape that is rare on Long Island, but widely used in other parts of the world from the Vouvray region of France to South Africa.

From their European and Middle Eastern backgrounds, the Massouds know that building a winery is a long and arduous task. Echoing a sentiment often expressed by wine growers, Ursula Massoud says, "You have to be in love with what you are doing, otherwise you couldn't stand it." Charles adds, "Grape growing teaches humility and patience. Our work will only pay back in the second generation, when our children have their children." It is this combination of passionate commitment and old world, wine culture that gives Paumanok its high promise.

Paumanok Vineyards

Main Road

Aquebogue, New York 11931

(516) 722-8800

VISITING:

Open: 11 AM – 6 PM, Weekends.
11 AM – 5PM, Weekdays. Closed
Monday – Tuesday, October – April.
Access for disabled provided.

Format for tastings: No charge.

Retail shop accepts Mastercard, Visa,
American Express. Picnic area
provided.

Special events: Fall, Harvest Festival; Early Summer, Introduction of new wines;
December, Barrel Tasting of new reds. Schedule announced yearly.

THE VINEYARD: 50 acres

Grape Varieties: Chardonnay (34%), Riesling (22%), Sauvignon Blanc (5%),
Chenin Blanc (3%), Cabernet Sauvignon (20%), Merlot (13%), Cabernet
Franc (3%).

THE WINES:

Chardonnay, Riesling, Riesling Dry, Riesling Semi-Dry, Chenin Blanc, Cabernet
Sauvignon, Merlot.

PERSONNEL:

Owners: Charles And Ursula Massoud

Vineyard Manager: Ursula Massoud

Winemaker: Charles Massoud

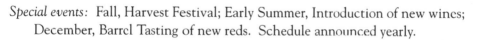

North Fork of Long Island
CHENIN BLANC
1991
Dry Table Wine

Produced and Bottled by
PAUMANOK Vineyards, Ltd., Aquebogue, NY 11931.

11.5% Alcohol by Volume

Ron Goerler, Jr., and Ron Goerler, Sr., Jamesport Vineyards.

Jamesport Winery

The barn that was reconstructed to become Jamesport Vineyards winery was built almost 150 years ago. In what used to be the hayloft, one beam is carved with the names, Wayne and Abby, 1858. They probably were too preoccupied, blissfully one imagines, to conceive of the reincarnation of their potato barn as a winery. On another beam, two of the builders, Lefty Goldsmith and Wayne Tuttle, proudly left their names. This pride is reflected in Ronald Goerler and his son, Ronald Jr., as they labor to build a second life for Jamesport.

The history of Jamesport Vineyards is a reminder, as if anyone in the region really needs it, of the risks that accompany the winemaking business. Established in 1980 as Northfork Winery by an out-of-state holding company, it encompassed one of the largest and most varied vineyards on Long Island. However, the financial resources of the corporation were unable to support the cash requirements of wine production on the scale planned, and by 1986 it shattered into bankruptcy. Ron Goerler, an experienced businessman, was brought in at that time to pick up the pieces and guide the ailing corporation through Chapter Eleven proceedings. In return he obtained a majority share of the corporation's stock. In the end, the property had to be liquidated. Ron obtained full title to the barn and a few adjacent acres, but not to the vineyards themselves, which remained in other hands. This did not deter Goerler. He was already owner of some sixty acres in nearby Cutchogue, forty of which had been planted to grapes in 1982. Here was a vineyard without a winery and a winery without vines. The two came together as Jamesport Vineyards in 1989.

Ron is evidently a canny businessman as well as a wine lover. After a three year hiatus, Jamesport is fully operational again. Coming from an entrepreneurial background, including the ownership of a successful plumbing manufacturing company, he has adopted a tough fiscal stance to ensure that the winery remains a viable enterprise. As Ron puts it, "From a business side, I always like to make money.... You have to have that in mind, otherwise its only a hobby."

The vineyards in Cutchogue are a patchwork quilt of several varietals managed by Ron, Jr. There are minuscule plots of Riesling, Semillon and Cabernet Franc, in addition to the ubiquitous Merlot, Cabernet Sauvignon and Chardonnay. There is also some Pinot Noir, used to make a champagne-style sparkling wine, and Sauvignon Blanc. The cultivation of this last varietal is especially interesting since it has been conspicuously unsuccessful on Long Island, enough so that several vineyards in the area have torn out their early plantings of this grape and replaced it with other varietals. However, the Goerlers believe that a fine Sauvignon Blanc can be grown here, since it seems to work well in the viticulturally similar area of Bordeaux. They argue that its conspicuous lack of success until now may be due to poor clones and inappropriately chosen planting sites, and they are determined to rectify this.

In a further attempt to distinguish themselves from the competition, the Goerlers are producing a Chardonnay more reminiscent of a wine from the Chablis region of France than of Burgundy. Most wineries aim to make a Burgundian style Chardonnay, rich textured and creamy, and few opt for a leaner, more focused wine. After several trips to the winemaking regions of France, the Goerlers have come to prefer the bone dry texture and mineral, almost flinty, scents of a fine Chablis. In part this is due to the soil of this small region of France, but it is also a question of vinification. By fermenting in stainless steel they manage to produce a Chardonnay that shares some of the stony quality of authentic Chablis. Both the zingy Sauvignon Blanc, and crisp Chardonnay are perfect foils for the abundant shellfish catch from coastal waters of the North Fork. This may be yet another manifestation of the cliché that the wines of a vineyard region always seem to match the cuisine of that area.

The winemaking at Jamesport is done by Ron, Jr. with the help of consultants. "They orchestrate it, and we do the grunt work," says Ron, half joking, but the final product is strictly a family decision, especially the final blending from different vats. "We know what we like, and we do the blending."

At the moment the Goerlers are in a phase of fine tuning the vineyards, which include some of the highest slopes in the appellation (forty to fifty feet above sea level) by trying to match varietals to terrain. They too believe that ultimately, the quality of a wine is limited by circumstances in the fields, among the rows of vines.

Jamesport Vineyards

P.O. Box 842

Main Road

Jamesport, N.Y. 11947

Phone (516) 722-5256

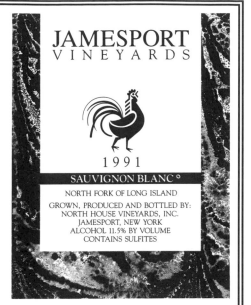

VISITING:

Open: 10 AM – 5PM, Monday – Saturday, May – January. 12 Noon – 5 PM, Sunday. Self-guided tours. Access for disabled provided.

Format for tastings: No charge.

Retail shop accepts Mastercard, Visa. Picnic area provided.

THE VINEYARD: 40 acres

Grape Varieties: Chardonnay (30%), Sauvignon Blanc (12.5%), Riesling (2.5%), Semillon (2.5%), CabernetSauvignon (12.5%), Merlot (12.5%), Pinot Noir (7.5%), Cabernet Franc (5%), Gamay Noir (5%).

THE WINES:

Chardonnay, Three Barrel Select Chardonnay, Sauvignon Blanc, Riesling, Cabernet Sauvignon, Merlot, Gamay Noir, Méthode Champenoise Sparkling Wine.

PERSONNEL:

Owners: Ron and Anne Marie Goerler, Sr.

Vineyard Manager: Ron Goerler, Jr.

Winemaker: Ron Goerler, Jr.

John and Richard Simicich, Mattituck Hills Winery.

Mattituck Hills Winery

The sparsely populated farmlands that lie below the Mattituck Hills, a stretch of bluffs that overlook Long Island Sound, shelter the neatly tended vineyards of John and Cathy Simicich, owners of the appropriately named Mattituck Hills Winery. Their home is surrounded by a white picket fence enclosing a profusion of plants and trees that provide a dense oasis in the dusty scrubland that lies beyond the vines. John says that Cathy loves trees so he planted at least one of every tree he could find in the area's nurseries, creating a miniature arboretum. Several dogs and cats, along with a corral of prized horses, complete the picture of a self-contained homestead. Just down the road, at the corner of Sound Avenue, is the new winery and spacious, dusty pink tasting room. Opened in 1991, the winery includes kitchen facilities for food and wine events, such as a series of wine dinners and cooking classes showcasing Mattituck Hills wines.

The verdant, peaceful scene of farm house and winery belies the risk-filled struggle through which many Long Island vineyards have passed. As with many of their peers on Long Island, the Simicichs stretched themselves financially and emotionally to pursue their calling. When they decided to add a winery to their grape growing operation, they sold virtually all their assets, including annuities and pensions, and negotiated a significant loan through Suffolk County to come up with the three quarters of a million dollars they needed to build and equip the winery. Their reputation as growers of superior grapes allowed them to continue to sell grapes, receiving badly needed income while wine sales built up.

Like other North Fork wineries, Mattituck Hills is a family enterprise, combining the efforts of three daughters, a son and a son-in-law. They produce Chardonnay, Riesling, Cabernet Sauvignon, Merlot and Pinot Noir. In spite of a successful 1988 vintage, John is considering phasing out the Riesling due to its poor ripening in off years. Wineries in upstate New York are more and more cognizant of the superior quality of grapes from Eastern Long Island, and the Simicichs have no problem selling as much as they want, currently about half their production. Their eventual goal is to dedicate the production of their entire forty acres to Mattituck Hills estate wines.

John Simicich is a self-taught winemaker who learned the basics as a young boy in New York City from his Yugoslavian-born father. John helped his father make quantities of wine for their extended family from grapes bought in the marketplace. Later, after moving out to Long Island, he was inspired by the example of the Hargraves and others. He started planting grapes in 1983. With the help of cooperative education wine seminars, reference books and the friendly advice of other winemakers, John gradually evolved into the winemaker of today. A builder by profession, he constructed both his home and the winery. To make ends meet, he is still active in the construction business. Despite his Yugoslavian ancestry, John has the unmistakable outdoors look of a Burgundian grape grower. He would not look out of place in the vineyards of Montrachet or Santenay.

Cathy Simicich, in addition to participating in the multitude of chores around the vineyard and winery, not to mention her own house and garden, was at one time President of the Long Island Wine Growers' Association. She is now active in that organization's successor, the Long Island Wine Council. In part because it acts as a recipient for New York State matching funds, the Wine Council has somewhat miraculously been effective in bringing together Long Island's very individualistic winemakers and vineyard owners to promote the region's wines.

The Simicichs' first crop (Chardonnay) was harvested in 1986 and was sold upstate. Although they made a small amount of wine for their own use in 1986, their first commercial wine was a Cabernet Sauvignon from the 1987 vintage. By 1990, Mattituck Hills was selling several wines from the excellent 1988 vintage: a distinctive and flavorful Riesling, a Chardonnay and a Cabernet Sauvignon aged in American oak. John is especially pleased with the reception given to his Cabernets, which he considers his signature wines. The 1988 has been a constant favorite with visitors at the tasting room, rivaled only by the tasty Merlot. The full-blown, barrel fermented Chardonnay of 1991 also established Mattituck Hills as a serious contender in the world of Long Island Chardonnays.

Mattituck Hills Winery

150 Bergen Avenue
Mattituck, New York 11952
(516) 298-9150

MATTITUCK HILLS
NORTH FORK OF LONG ISLAND, NEW YORK

Pinot Noir
BLANC DE NOIR

1 9 9 1

GROWN, PRODUCED AND BOTTLED BY
MATTITUCK HILLS WINERY INC., MATTITUCK, NEW YORK

NET CONTENTS 750 ML
ALCOHOL 11.5% BY VOLUME   CONTAINS SULFITES

VISITING:

Open: 11 AM – 6 PM, May – December.
11 AM – 5PM, January – April. Access
for disabled provided.

Format for tastings: No charge.

Retail shop accepts Mastercard, Visa,
American Express. Picnic area with
deck with tables and chairs.

Special events: Wine dinners with guest chef.
Please call for details.

THE VINEYARD: 40 acres

Grape Varieties: Chardonnay (37%), Cabernet Sauvignon (25%), Merlot (25%),
Pinot Noir (10%), Riesling (3%).

THE WINES:

Chardonnay, Chardonnay Reserve, Riesling, Cabernet Sauvignon, Merlot, Pinot
Noir Blanc de Noir, Mattituck Red.

PERSONNEL:

Owners: John and Cathy Simicich

Vineyard Manager: Richard Simicich

Winemaker: John Simicich

Assistant Winemaker: Tom Zaweski

Sales and Promotion Manager: Cathy Simicich

Tasting Room and Sales: Joanne Simicich and Christine Zaweski

Tour Guide: Stephanie Simicich

Peconic Bay Vineyards

A visitor to the North Fork is conditioned to look for wineries along the north side of Main Road, Route 25, where eight of them are located. Therefore, it comes as something of a jolt to see the tasting room and vines of Peconic Bay Vineyards on the south side of the road in the center of Cutchogue. A converted farmhouse serves as a wine storage area, tasting room and home to Ray Blum, the owner. Nearby are renovated potato sheds that house the winery itself. The thirty acres of surrounding vineyards, with a rosebush at the end of each row, were purchased by Ray in 1979, but the first wine was not made until 1984. Until then he sold his grapes. However, the uncertainties of grape growing included a fluctuating marketplace.

Charles Flatt and Ray Blum, Peconic Bay Vineyards.

Buyers were accustomed to setting their own prices and to changing the amount they would purchase from year to year. To avoid doing business this way, he began to use the facilities at Lenz to vinify all the grapes that he could not profitably sell. Today his conversion from grape seller to winemaker is total, including the use of grapes that he cultivates on another twenty-seven acres of leased land. Since 1989 he has done all his winemaking on his own premises.

Ray recalls reading about grape growing in a magazine in mid-December, 1978. He admits to being driven to accomplish new and different things, and he bought the vineyard just three months later. Having a degree in horticulture certainly helped the decision to buy the property, and being "a hands-on kind of guy," as he describes himself, Ray does a lot of the day to day work with the help of a vineyard manager and winemaker, Charles Flatt. In between, he works as an air-traffic controller for the Federal Aviation Commission. He also services a number of other wineries during grape picking with his large mechanical harvester. At one time Blum did landscape contracting and planted and managed vineyards for others. Today, in addition to the harvesting operations, Blum leases out and services a state-of-the-art bottling tractor to other wineries that cannot afford to invest in this essential item of cellar equipment.

Blum's production centers on Cabernet Sauvignon, Cabernet Franc, Merlot, Chardonnay and Riesling. He has a considerable amount of Riesling planted, which is used to make a dry and flavorful white wine as well as a late harvest dessert wine called

Vin de L'Ile-Blanc. Additionally, Riesling is part of the blend for a blush wine. The Chardonnay is produced in up to three different types, depending on the vintage; from a crisp stainless-steel fermented wine to a more unctuous barrel fermented version. He does not consciously try to conform to any preconceived benchmark, and his wines have a style all their own, especially the Chardonnay which is smooth and rich.

It all begins in the vineyard, where hedging opens the leaf canopy to light and air. Careful pruning controls the number of buds on a cane and, consequently, the number of clusters obtained. Crop thinning and leaf removal are used more sparingly. Later, in the cellar, Ray employs a variety of different barrels, including American oak, to increase the complexity of the wines.

Most, if not all, of the wineries are gradually expanding their production, and Ray feels that new plantings are inevitable, since the current supply of grapes no longer satisfies the demand. This has been evident from the decline in the number of grapes sold outside the appellation and the increase in the number of acres that wineries lease. Peconic Bay is very much part of this expansion, which expresses the confidence Ray Blum has in the future of the region.

Peconic Bay Vineyards

P.O. Box 709

Main Road, Route 25

Cutchogue, N.Y. 11935

Phone (516) 734-7361

VISITING:

Open: 11 AM – 5 PM, Daily. No Access
for disabled.

Format for Tastings: No Charge.

Retail shop accepts Mastercard, Visa.
Picnic area provided.

THE VINEYARD: 57 acres

Grape Varieties: Chardonnay, Riesling, Merlot, Cabernet Sauvignon, Cabernet Franc.

THE WINES:

Chardonnay Reserve, Estate Chardonnay, Petite Chardonnay, White Riesling,
Vin de L'Ile Blanc, Blush, Cabernet Sauvignon, Merlot, Cabernet Franc.

PERSONNEL:

Owner: Ray Blum

Winemaker: Charles Flatt

Joyce and Bob Pellegrini, Pellegrini Vineyards.

Pellegrini Vineyards

The gazebo just off the main street in Cutchogue used to be a familiar sight to visitors touring the North Fork. Recently, however, it was removed as groundbreaking began for the newest arrival to this appellation, Pellegrini Vineyards. Although the winery is new, the vineyards are not. Bob Pellegrini, a graphic arts designer with his own firm in New York City, has a long association with this area.

Bob and his wife Joyce, a retired schoolteacher, first considered the possibility of a vineyard in 1981. Like other newcomers of that period, he sought the advice of the Hargraves, talked to David Mudd, then the impressario of vineyards, and looked for land. Eventually he joined forces with Jerry Gristina and together they bought the fifty acre parcel that is now Gristina Vineyards. The partnership did not last, however, and Bob went off looking for new possibilities. After a long lapse, he finally closed on a thirty-six acre site in 1991 that, as luck would have it, is right next door to Gristina.

Originally known as Island Vineyards, the parcel had vines on it that were planted by Mudd in 1982 for the previous owners. Even though Pellegrini was late in arriving on the scene, the availability of mature vines on his property gave him a jump start. The 1992 vintage will probably be his first.

Thirty of the acres are planted in Chardonnay, Cabernet Sauvignon and Merlot, and while some older vines of Pinot Noir are being torn out, there are new rows of Cabernet Franc to replace them. The vines have been retrained to low wires on the undulating, sandy soil. The porous soil gives excellent drainage, but as Bob points out, in arid growing seasons such as 1991, some of the vines can be stressed excessively. Fortunately, a drip irrigation system is in place that can be a boon in such unusual years.

When asked why he ever got into this business, Bob chuckled as he answered with a familiar refrain among winery owners: "You can make money in much better investments than a vineyard.... You have to love it and just want to do it."

When the winery building is complete, it will consist of three sections surrounding a courtyard and connected by walkways. Bob and Joyce expect to use it as a showcase for their wine, and they will host food and wine events.

Pellegrini's winemaker is Russell Hearn, formerly at Le Rève. Russell received his first vinicultural training with Houghton's Vineyard in Australia where he started as an apprentice in 1978. After five years with Houghton, he spent a short period in Burgundy and a year in California. There he met his wife-to-be who caused him to stay in the United States. His light lilting Australian accent has been tempered by four years spent as the winemaker at Commonwealth Vineyards in Massachusetts, and softened by a couple of years in Culpeper, Virginia, where he was winemaker with Dominion Wine Cellars. His speech is remarkably precise. Each syllable of each word is distinct. It is a pleasure to hear him pronounce words such as "opportunity" and "absolutely" and to hear him construct thoughtfully complete sentences which begin and end as cleanly as a well controlled fermentation.

Although Russell had been an interested and knowledgeable observer of the Long Island wine scene for a number of years, it was only in the late 1980s that he felt the region showed unambiguous promise. Soon after, he made his decision to move to the region.

Russell's approach to winemaking is as controlled and precise as his speech. His emphasis on control relates to his view of tradition in winemaking which, he says, is a typical Australian view. Traditional practices should be employed if, and only if, they are shown to work reliably and have some technical justification, not because they have always been used. "I try to use tradition with as much technology as possible," he says.

Some winemakers on Long Island believe in a non-interventionist approach to winemaking. Russell Hearn is just the opposite. He is a careful, risk averse, technocratic winemaker. He says he does not believe in "dirty wines," which seems like a peculiar thing to have to say. Does anyone believe in dirty wines?

As it turns out, they do. For example, Eric Fry at Lenz Vineyards speaks with admiring intent about "dirty, barnyardy, funky wines." This is the winespeak that Eric uses to describe what are quite subtle qualities of some of the great, red wines of Burgundy. They are qualities attained though traditional techniques and procedures, such as fermenting with a large percentage of solids and the use of minimum filtration. This approach can be risky, however, for one false step and the barnyard will overwhelm the wine, and a whole vintage will be lost.

Richard Olsen-Harbich at Bridgehampton is willing to initiate his fermentation with the wild yeasts that come in with the harvested grapes. Russell, on the other hand, says he will never in his life allow a wine to be made with a natural yeast. Why take the risk? Olsen-Harbich and Fry would argue that it is by taking risk that you make it possible to make a great wine. Of course it is also possible to have a complete failure, a possibility that Russell wants to avoid at almost any cost. "I want to minimize my chances of things going wrong," he says. "My job as a professional winemaker is to never make a bad wine."

Russell's objective goes well beyond simply avoiding bad wines. He has very definite ideas of the qualities he wants to produce in his wines, and precisely how to produce them. Primarily, his objective is to reveal the qualities of the fresh grapes and secondarily, to add complexity. He wants to avoid "hitting the fruit over the head." Thus, he uses new oak barrels advisedly for his Chardonnay; he wants the influence of the oak without an oak flavor.

Pellegrini Vineyards

23005 Main Road
Cutchogue, N.Y. 11932
Phone (516) 734-4111
Fax (516) 734-4159

VISITING:

Open: 10 AM – 5:30 PM, Daily. Self-guided tours. Private tours by appointment. Access for disabled provided.

Retail shop accepts Mastercard, Visa, American Express. Picnic area provided.

Special events: Please call for details.

THE VINEYARD: 30 acres

Grape Varieties: Chardonnay (45%), Merlot (23%), Cabernet Sauvignon (20%), Cabernet Franc (6%), Pinot Noir (6%).

THE WINES:

First Release: Spring, 1993

Chardonnay, Cabernet Sauvignon, Merlot, House White.

PERSONNEL:

Owners: Bob and Joyce Pellegrini

Vineyard Manager: Chris Kelly

Winemaker: Russell Hearn

Patricia Pugliese, Pugliese Vineyards.

Pugliese Vineyards

Nestled comfortably between the vineyards of Ressler and Pindar is Pugliese Vineyards, until recently, the smallest winery of them all. A handsome burgundy colored sign on Route 25A beckons the visitor to the tasting room which lies behind a country house that is destined to become a restaurant. One is welcomed by a pair of well fed mallards that waddle out of a small pond beside the winery and accompany the visitor inside, presumably for something more satisfying to drink than pond water.

Ralph and Patricia Pugliese, with their sons and daughters, have made this a family enterprise ever since arriving in 1980. Although it was supposed to be their vacation home, planting two acres of grapes in their first year seemed to be a natural thing to do. "I've been making wine since I was ten years old," says Ralph. He was raised in Brooklyn at a time when fathers and uncles made wine at home from grapes purchased in the market, and young family members joined in. Later, when he gave up his job as president of a construction union, the old Brooklyn traditions were taken east to a more bucolic setting.

The Puglieses have a style all their own. Their popular Blanc de Blanc champenoise sparkling wine boasts elaborately hand painted bottles, each painstakingly crafted by Patricia. The vineyards not only include the usual Chardonnay, Merlot, and Cabernet, but also plantings of Zinfandel. An experimental blend of Zinfandel, Cabernet Sauvignon and Cabernet Franc is in the works. In addition, they grow tomatoes which are turned into sauces that, quite likely, will grace the kitchen of the new restaurant where Ralph will reign as chef.

Grapes are hand picked at Pugliese, and the wines undergo malolactic fermentation at cool temperatures. Barrel aging of both white and red wines takes place in American oak. A recently tasted three year old Chardonnay was ripe and flavorful, with a buttery texture and hints of spice in the nose. In spite of their small size, Pugliese has been visible on the North Fork wine scene ever since their first vintage in 1986, and their well crafted wines now occupy a central role in the appellation.

Pugliese Vineyards

Main Road, Route 25
Cutchogue, N.Y. 11935
Phone (516) 734-4057

VISITING:

Open: 11 AM – 5 PM. Access for
　disabled:.

Format for Tastings: No Charge.

Retail shop: accepts Mastercard, Visa,
　American Express. No Picnic area.

THE VINEYARD: 22.5 acres

Grape Varieties: Chardonnay (36.4%),
　Merlot (31.8%), Cabernet
　Sauvignon (31.8%).

THE WINES:

Chardonnay, Chardonnay Gold, Chardonnay Blush, Merlot, Cabernet
　Sauvignon, Champagne Blanc de Blanc.

PERSONNEL:

Owner: Patricia Pugliese

Winemaker: Ralph Pugliese

Vineyard Manager: Peter Pugliese

ESTATE BOTTLED
1988

Pugliese Vineyards

Chardonnay

NORTH FORK OF LONG ISLAND

GROWN, PRODUCED AND BOTTLED BY
PUGLIESE VINEYARDS
CUTCHOGUE, L.I. NEW YORK
ALC. 11.5 BY VOLUME

Harry and John Mariani, Banfi Vineyards at Old Brookville.

Banfi

The Banfi vineyard is altogether atypical of Long Island. There are no converted potato barns and rustic tasting rooms here. A somber, unmarked gate swings open off Cedar Swamp Road in the exclusive residential area of Old Brookville in Nassau County to usher a visitor into the palatial estate. A long road winds past 127 immaculately kept acres of rolling meadow and woodland until it reaches the manor house, once owned by the widow of Alfred Vanderbilt. The Elizabethan style mansion, with its slate roofs and cobblestone courtyards, is now the corporate headquarters of the vast Banfi wine empire. Just beyond the house are the vineyards: fifty-five acres of high density plantings of Chardonnay. One is struck by the similarity to the great châteaux of Bordeaux, the Loire or Champagne that hover over their celebrated vineyards.

No wine is made at the Old Brookville estate. Instead, a select number of hand picked grapes are quickly trucked upstate to the Château Frank winery in Hammondsport, to be vinified into a regular Chardonnay and a Blanc de Blanc sparkling wine. The rest of the grapes are harvested and then crushed at one of several North fork wineries, to be later sold as grape juice to any number of other wineries.

Total production is small, averaging somewhat over 2,000 cases, and distribution is largely limited to the New York City area. In spite of an aggressive sales force, the Old Brookville vineyards are in truth a minor corporate interest at Banfi, whose worldwide holdings dwarf the Long Island enterprise. In Montalcino, Italy, for example, an enormous wine estate releases a wide array of wines including the prestigious and much awarded Brunello di Montalcino. Apparently, the main reason for the Long Island vineyard is to keep fifty-five acres of prime land in a rural state and out of the hands of developers; a shrewd public relations move that endears Banfi to the surrounding community. It is also an ornament, a charming conceit, to maintain the illusion of a titled estate. The mansion astride rolling fields and vines enhances the corporate image. It titillates the frequent guests and serves, additionally, to give the sales staff a first hand taste of viticulture.

The vineyards were the idea of the Banfi owners, John and Harry Mariani, who did the first plantings in 1983 after they purchased an adjacent property, then known as Young's Farms. Shortly thereafter, they hired Fred Frank, a Cornell graduate trained in practical viticulture at Geisenheim, Germany. It is Fred's father who owns the winery in Hammondsport that turns the Old Brookville grapes into wine. Moreover, the acclaimed Dr. Konstantin Frank, who first successfully introduced vinifera grapes to a skeptical wine industry in upper New York State, is Fred's grandfather. Dr. Frank was instrumental in persuading Alex Hargrave to come to Long Island. After Dr. Frank's death, Eric Fry, now winemaker at Lenz, took his position. It is intriguing to note how the Banfi vines are entwined with the story of Long Island wines.

Harry Mariani said that plans are ready for a winery at the Old Brookville estate, but construction is on hold until they are convinced that there is more of a market for the wines. "Its a tough sell," says Harry of his Chardonnay, because of the enormous competition.

It also takes all the skill and dedication of Fred Frank to cultivate the grapes in an area that has a shorter growing season than the North Fork. As a consultant to the upstate family winery, he opts for a "leaner, cleaner style of Chardonnay, more Chablis-like than Macon." On the other hand, the sparkling Blanc de Blanc that ages three years on its yeasts (the 1986 vintage was released in 1990, the next vintage was produced in 1990) is an impressive méthode champenoise bubbly, with toasty and complex flavors.

Banfi Vineyards at Old Brookville

1111 Cedar Swamp Road
Old Brookville, N.Y. 11545
Phone (516) 626-9200
Fax (516) 626-9218

VISITING:

Not open to the public.

THE VINEYARD: 55 acres

Grape Varieties: Chardonnay (100%).

THE WINES:

Chardonnay, Blanc de Blancs.

PERSONNEL:

Owners: John and Harry Mariani

Vineyard Manager: Frederick Frank

Winemaker: Custom bottled at Château Frank, Hammondsport, N.Y.

Dave Mudd, North Fork Wine Services.

CHAPTER 5

Supporting Cast

And Noah began to be a husbandman, and he planted a vineyard. And he drank of the wine.
— Genesis

The wineries, their owners and winemakers are the principal actors in the story of wine on Long Island. However, there are also a number of supporting roles in this cast; perhaps less visible to the public at large, but nonetheless crucial.

To begin with, the staff of the wineries play indispensable roles, from working the fields to conducting tours. Beyond these largely unsung people, there are many others who assist in bringing wine to center stage. From a wide spectrum of activities, we have chosen to highlight four diverse individuals who are inextricably woven into the fabric of our story.

One, David Mudd, has been advisor and consultant to neophyte wineries as well as to those well established. Mudd has provided services in clearing land, staking rows upon rows of new vineyard sites, providing rootstocks, supplying barrels and equipment, managing existing winery operations, and even distributing the bottled wine to clients. His role as factotum has made him an invaluable resource on the North Fork.

Then there is Alice Wise, technical advisor and viticultural troubleshooter, who visits the fields to diagnose problems. From her office at the Cornell Cooperative Extension Service, she provides nostrums for ailing vines. Her research into plant pathology and clonal selection is the foundation for the vineyards of the future.

Ressler vineyards, a name unrecognized by the public because it does not appear on any label, is nevertheless well known to the several wineries that buy grapes from this carefully tended vineyard. Kirk Ressler and his brother Richard, do not make any wine, but sell their prized fruit to others. For wineries with limited land to cultivate, the purchase of grapes is an essential, if little acknowledged, part of the business. Although there are other grape growers who sell all their crop, it is the Ressler name that most often seems to come to the fore in discussions with winemakers.

The wines of Long Island ultimately appear on the consumer's table because of the support of the many retailers in the New York metropolitan area who have put the bottles on their shelves. Some of the more celebrated dining establishments have also placed the wines on their lists, side by side with prestigious bottles from other parts of the world. What better way is there for the public to gain confidence in a wine than to see it appear on the roster of acclaimed restaurants and inns throughout the region. From a long list of restaurants we have chosen Ross' North Fork Restaurant in Southold. Chef-owner John Ross has a long association with North Fork wines, beginning long before they became chic. He has enthusiastically promoted them on his premises, and vineyard owners speak of him with respect and affection.

The list of individuals who play an indisputably significant role in the region could go on and on, but we cannot leave this introduction without mentioning Cynthia Fuller and Phil Nugent. Cynthia was mentioned earlier as Kip Bedell's marketing director. Although connected with Bedell, Cynthia is also identified with the aspirations of the region as a whole. She enthusiastically offers her experience and advice to the myriad wine promoting events that take place at restaurants throughout the New York metropolitan region. She is a key participant in charity fund raisers as well, and helped make Stony Brook University's Annual Food and Wine event a successful scholarship drive.

Phil Nugent, sometime advisor and consultant to Bridgehampton and Lenz wineries, is the low-key, but accomplished director of the Long Island Wine Council: the official promotional arm of the industry. In this role as "ambassador at large" he has been instrumental in effectively organizing important media events, including the annual Windows on Long Island at the Windows on the World in Manhattan.

North Fork Wine Services

The entrepreneurial do-it-all of the Long Island wine industry is an affable, but no-nonsense former airline pilot, David Mudd. Tall and rugged, Dave has been on the scene nearly as long as the Hargraves, providing a host of ancillary services to a growing community of grape growers, leading the way in innovative technology and advising those who listen, as well as those who do not.

The current hub of all his activity is a large, 200,000-case warehouse on Route 105 in Riverhead. Under the name of North Fork Wine Services, it provides temperature and humidity controlled storage facilities for wineries and private collectors. It is also the distribution point for the delivery of wine to retailers and restaurants, and of prestigious Seguin Moreau oak barrels from France to winemakers.

He started in 1974 with one acre of land in Southold that ultimately expanded to the current thirty-six acre Mudd Vineyards which he holds jointly with his son, Steve. Soon after arriving, he called on his previous background in farming and began to consult with the inexperienced and often absentee vineyard owners who were beginning to appear. He cleared their land, installed the poles and wires, supplied the vine cuttings, did the plantings, and provided the maintenance services that were needed. With a graft cutter purchased early on, he did thousands of graftings in those years. Pindar, Lenz, Jamesport, Island Vineyards (now Pellegrini), Palmer and others availed themselves of Mudd's expertise. Palmer, in particular, has had a close association with him, especially since Mudd supervised the construction and opening of the winery.

Although new plantings have become less frequent lately, the maintenance services continue unabated, as does his introduction of innovative contrivances to simplify the job of vineyard management. The latest is a mechanical vine lifter to raise up the trellis wires during the growing season as the canopy becomes laden with growth. This serves to expose the fruit to light and to thin out the foliage, a labor-intensive task that can now be done much more efficiently. Similarly, he introduced a leaf plucker and hedger from New Zealand that does that job more quickly. Then there is the drip irrigation system, a favorite topic with Mudd ever since he installed the first ones at Island Vineyards in 1982 and at Palmer in 1983. While others may complain about the problems of rainfall and excess humidity that breed rot and fungal diseases, Dave will extol the virtues of trickle irrigation, citing the relatively low cost of installation and the inestimable advantages it confers to a vineyard during a drought. He cites the example of Palmer Vineyards where there are parcels of land that would suffer irreversible damage were it not for the availability of water. When reminded of the cliché that vines need to be stressed to provide good fruit, he replies that that is just a rationalization on the part of vineyard owners who don't already own an irrigation system. As for humidity and rot, Dave is quick to retort that his leaf plucker will expose the fruit to drying breezes.

Mudd has spearheaded a succession of initiatives to bring new investments into the North and South forks to offset the adverse impact of a 1985 change in the tax laws that reduced a number of favorable tax writeoffs. In particular, the new laws require an absentee owner to be an active participant in the vineyard operations in order to take a loss. This has slowed the momentum of growth, and the 1,400 or so acres that were under development in 1985 have not increased much since. Dave feels that 10,000 vineyard acres would make more sense. In concert with others, he has attempted to lure a large winery operation to the area, especially a foreign investor, who would give a much needed spurt to the economy and attract other investors. So far, these initiatives have not succeeded, though some did look promising for a while.

Because of his early start in the area, and his intimate knowledge of the day-to-day operations of many of the wineries, Dave is exceptionally well informed about the comings and goings on the two forks. Moreover, he is not shy about voicing his opinions, which are interspersed with amusing anecdotes. In discussing the relations between local farmers and the newly arrived vineyard owners, he quips, "Sure, there is friction to the extent that we're the guys with the lace pants, and they're the ones with the sacks on their asses because they're going out of business. The banks won't lend them any more money. They are dead in the water." Then he will launch into a discussion of the economics and shortcomings of potato farming in Suffolk County.

He may also tell the story of John Wickham, when he brought down celebrated wine-maker Konstantin Frank from upstate for a meeting in Riverhead. With Wickham's permission, Frank brought a tremendous vinifera grape vine with huge roots grown by Wickham. "I'm going to say what I'm going to say, even with John here. He's been giving this big plant here lots to eat. The problem is that it's like a person who needs a chicken leg to eat, and you make him eat the whole chicken." John got up, chuckled and said, "I don't disagree with you, but in my farm stand people want nice big grapes and that's what I have to give them." As Dave wryly comments, this is the first lesson in the difference between grapes for the table and grapes for wine.

Speaking of the latter, he sees the future in Merlot, Cabernet Franc, and Chardonnay. The other varietals, he feels, either do not grow well, or do not sell well. Vintners should stick to what works. Another story he tells is of Soundview Vineyards in Peconic which, in an ill-advised move, planted twenty acres of the hybrid grape Seyval Blanc that just could not be sold. Dave's own experiences with peach growing as a side-line, convinced him that orchards were not economically viable, and they have all been bulldozed out.

Besides his obvious delight in the business of doing business, Dave's love is farming. "When I was a high school kid in Missouri," he muses, "I would go out on my relative's farm every weekend. It's something I liked to do and couldn't get enough of, and still enjoy." Dave does not plan to have a winery himself, since he does not want to compete with the people that he services. Smiling, he adds "Besides, why bother when all I have to do is go down the road to Palmer to get the few bottles I need."

Cornell Cooperative Extension Service of Long Island

Driving along Sound Avenue in the town of Riverhead, it is easy to be distracted by the scenic farmland and not notice the unassuming building that houses the Cornell Cooperative Extension Service of Long Island. The Cooperative Extension is a public service offshoot of Cornell University that disseminates research-based information to the farming industry on Long Island. The University, in upstate New York, has long been affiliated with agriculture, and its bulletins on pest control, soil conservation and the like are welcomed by many in the farming community.

Part of this service deals with viticulture, and the New York State Experimental Station in Geneva is a recognized source of information on vineyard management practices. The Long Island facility along Sound Avenue is, however, a more modest enterprise in which viticulture is represented by a single person, Alice Wise. She is a consultant to the wineries and singlehandedly runs educational programs and conferences, issues newsletters, and conducts research on issues of particular concern to the industry. With a degree in Horticulture from the University of Maryland, she did graduate work in the Pomology department at Cornell where she earned her degree with a thesis on pest management.

Alice Wise, Cornell Cooperative Extension Service of Long Island.

Concerning her current position in viticulture, Alice explains, "I was bitten by a bug [and became] consumed with interest about vineyards and winemaking."

When Alice took on the position of Viticultural Research Specialist at the beginning of 1991, one of her unexpected tasks was to overcome some of the skepticism of Long Island growers who felt that they had been misled by the upstate specialists into adopting viticultural practices ill-suited to the Island. The Cornell experts offered what they then knew, a decade or so ago. Much of their viticultural experience was gleaned from upstate, where climate and soil are vastly different from the North Fork. Their knowledge was also limited to native varietals or, at best, hybrids, whose requirements vary considerably from those of the European vinifera that have been planted since. To all accounts she has been persuasive by virtue of her intelligence and tact.

Although issues of vine nutrition, pruning and trellising methods and insect control are all of concern to grape growers, the Extension Service has chosen, under Alice's guidance, to focus initially on two questions of particular interest to the industry. One concerns the eradication, or at least the control, of crown gall, a bacterial infection that attacks vines weakened by winter damage. This is especially prevalent among plants grown in low lying areas where cold air masses collect. The disease manifests itself by abnormal growth that chokes and then kills the vine. One solution is to avoid planting in less desirable sites, where frost is prevalent. For many this is a difficult choice, economically at least, and an alternative approach is to find a way of inhibiting the bacterial infection.

Another line of research concerns a systematic evaluation of grape clones. There are, for example, more than a half dozen Chardonnay clones that differ in flavor, as well as in cluster size, ripening times and ability to resist certain diseases. In earlier years, grapes were planted on Long Island using whatever clonal types were commercially available, without much thought being given to their suitability. However, as Alice remarks, different clones planted on the same site make different wines. Various clones are now being evaluated in experimental plantings on a bit more than an acre of land just behind the quonset huts and hothouses that flank the Extension Service lab-office to see how they fare in Long Island climates and soils. The results could be significant in terms of identifying new clones that can produce wines of even greater character than those obtained from the clones selected rather haphazardly in the past. Some specialists feel that an important difference between the quality of Burgundian wines, and the Chardonnays and Pinot Noirs grown elsewhere, lies precisely in the choice of clone.

The decision to give priority to one research issue over another is reached in consultation with a Grape Advisory Committee made up of local growers and winemakers who help Alice set her research agenda. However, even though the fruits of her labors are available to all, at least one person has shrugged it off with the comment, "What can Cornell possibly tell me that I don't already know ?" Long experience with grape growing can teach someone "how to read a vineyard," as Alice puts it. However, few in this burgeoning but still fledgling region have yet acquired this uncommon wisdom. Alice adds, "Every vineyard has its own specific combination of soil types and landscape and none are the same." For this reason the Extension Service is likely to remain an important source of advice and support to the industry as it moves into the remainder of the decade.

Ressler Vineyards

A number of Long Island vineyards sell their grapes to other wineries instead of making wine themselves. Even though they are a less visible and certainly less glamorous part of the region's viticulture, they account for a sizable portion of the acres planted to vines on the north and south forks. We have chosen to write about just one of them, the highly regarded Ressler Vineyard of Cutchogue that began operating in 1981.

Hidden away from the main road, the Ressler vineyards appear unannounced, except for a modest sign near the end of a dirt path. A simple tool shed, a picnic bench under a shady tree and a frolicking dog are the only adornments for the forty-two acres of carefully tended rows of Chardonnay, Merlot, Cabernet Sauvignon and a bit of Sauvignon Blanc. Ben Sisson, the affable and expert vineyard manager, says that seven of the acres originally planted with Riesling were torn out to make room for more Merlot and some Cabernet Franc, since Riesling was deemed a few years ago not to be commercially viable.

The Ressler brothers, Richard and Kirk, sell their prized grapes to wineries up and down the Atlantic coast, and at least one winery has found it advantageous to announce on their label that the grapes are from Ressler Vineyards. There seems to be a consensus among the local winemakers that the quality of the fruit is consistently high. In part, this may be due to the fact that the Resslers have resisted the temptation to over-crop. The only sour note that intrudes from time to time is that a fastidious winemaker may object to the timing of the harvest. As Ben Sisson points out, many considerations contribute to the decision of when to pick, such as an impending rainstorm or the degree of ripeness of the grapes. At worst, such disagreements are marginal problems.

Kirk Ressler, a career diplomat, has logged a considerable amount of time in Europe for the State Department. While there, he was impressed by how deeply the cultivation of the vine is woven into the fabric of rural life. With a home on Shelter Island just off the North Fork, it is not surprising that he should have been drawn into planting his own vineyards. Having started without any prior experience in viticulture, however, the brothers eased themselves into the business of grapes and only recently began to feel that they were ready to make their own wine. "You can't make good wine until you have good grapes," explained Kirk.

It costs the Resslers about $2,000 per ton to grow grapes on the North Fork, and the wineries who buy them are reluctant to pay much more than that. The wholesale grape business runs on a low profit margin, whereas wine from the same grapes yields a higher return. For this reason, if none other, the Resslers have recently been talking to some of the existing wineries about forming a joint venture, and they may soon be making wine under their own label.

John Ross

In the bar of Ross' North Fork Restaurant is a shelf of cookbooks that range from the sublime to the ridiculous; from The Culinary Institute to the New York baseball team called GourMets. These tomes attest to the range and versatility of chef-owner John Ross, who is arguably the first, certainly the most venerable, of the several restauranteurs who have now committed themselves to the promotion of Long Island wines. Established in 1973, the same year that the Hargraves started up, John's restaurant offers local fare simply prepared and maintains a wine list that reflects his location: "right in the middle of wine country."

Ross straddles the culinary timeline. One foot is firmly planted in the 1950s, while the other is very much in the forefront of a new phenomenon in American cuisine: matching local bounty with the wines of the surrounding vineyards. Here one still finds celery and carrot sticks as openers in place of the herb-scented breads and sculpted canapes that are so trendy elsewhere. By contrast, his homemade breads, prepared by his pastry chef of many years, Bonnie Hoffer, impeccably fresh fish from Braun's market in Southold, and the succulent produce from nearby farm stands of Farmer Mike's, Wickham or Krupski, are presented as perfect foils to the array of wines on his impressive list.

Jaunty, alert and sincere, John looks younger than his age. When asked about his culinary background, he readily admits that it began quite modestly. He was born in Ontario, Canada, but he grew up in Dearborn, Michigan. He started to cook while he attended the University of Michigan. Ultimately, he dropped out of school to do full time cooking. After a four year stint in the Coast Guard, where he was a cooking instructor, John attended the Cornell Hotel School. After two years, he took a job at Squire's Restaurant in East Hampton, a fashionable and sophisticated place during the 1970s. While at Cornell he became interested in wine, including New York State wine. His knowledge broadened into French wines at Squire's.

Inevitably, in 1973, John opened his own restaurant on Route 25 in Southold. He remained there until 1984, when he moved to his current premises, also in Southold, but set back a bit off Route 48. His largest selling wine is the house wine, a blend of Chardonnay and Sauvignon Blanc that is especially made for him by Hargrave. Originally, the house wine was an inconsequential jug wine, like many restaurants still commonly serve, but he reflects, "I found myself serving food that I was proud of and wine that was garbage.... The quality of the house wine should be much higher than that." First with Pindar, and currently with Hargrave, he offered alternatives that set high standards.

Ross tries to maintain a library of older vintages of red wines, and during a recent visit, he uncorked a 1980 Hargrave Cabernet Sauvignon in excellent condition. It had deep flavors of plum, spice and cassis, with a lovely rich color. His kinship with the Hargraves extends back to the beginning when both were pioneers, and to prove it, he shows an old menu from 1975 that includes a selection from Hargrave. At present his wine list reads like a Who's Who of Long Island producers. It is no accident that the local winemakers go to Ross' when they hold their monthly discussion group. The discussion includes dinner and blind tastings of wine, but is closed to outsiders. The choice of meeting place is as much out of respect for what Ross has done for the wine community, as it is out of genuine fondness for his culinary skills.

John's motto, "keep it simple," is reflected in his recipe for lobster stew, given below. It is a summer favorite with his customers, and he suggests a full bodied, buttery Lenz Gold Label Chardonnay as "a match made in heaven." With other foods his matches would be different: Merlot with Long Island duckling; a crisp, stainless steel fermented, not barrel fermented Chardonnay for autumn fare, such as local pumpkin soup or cauliflower; and Sauvignon Blanc for oysters, cod or flounder caught off the Long Island coastline.

John looks confidently towards the future. As the Long Island appellations mature, he expects to be there as a standard bearer of regional cooking. His son Sanford, a recent engineering graduate of Clarkson, tends bar and seems to be following in his father's steps. John is not sure that he approves, but then he sheepishly recalls that when he dropped out of University to begin his career, his parents were also displeased.

Ross' Summer Lobster Stew

The following recipe is prefaced with John's advice for the ultimate trip: "Go out to the farm stands and wineries in the morning to shop; go home and cook all afternoon; and in the evening, on a deck overlooking the bay (or the Sound,) enjoy your efforts with good friends. It doesn't get any better than that."

8	live lobsters (1 1/4 lb. each)
4	strips bacon, diced
2	cups onion, diced
1	cup leeks, white part only, diced
1	cup green pepper, diced
1	cup red pepper, diced
2	tablespoons fresh thyme (or lemon thyme)
1	quart chicken broth
16	new potatoes, peeled, whole
8	ears fresh corn, scraped off cob
1	quart milk
4	ounces butter
4	ounces flour
1	tablespoon salt
1	teaspoon freshly ground pepper
1/4	cup chopped parsley

1. Boil lobsters until just cooked (about 18 minutes.) Remove meat from shells and cut into bite sized chunks.
2. Brown bacon in heavy stock pot.
3. Add onion , leek, peppers and thyme. Sweat until tender.
4. Add chicken broth and new potato. Cook until potatoes are just tender. Add corn and shut off heat.
5. In separate pan, make white sauce with milk and roux. It should be medium thickness. Season white sauce with salt and pepper.
6. Add white sauce to stock pot along with lobster chucks and chopped parsley. Bring just to the boil, check for seasoning, and serve. Serve in flat soup plates with crusty homemade bread.

Yield: 8 servings

Oak barrels, Hargrave Vineyard.

Chapter 6

Conclusion: Imaginary Balloons, Reputation & Romance

"In this wild spot [Napa Valley] I did not feel the sacredness of
ancient cultivation. It was still raw; it was no Marathon, and no
Johannisburg [sic]; yet the stirring sunlight, and the growing vines,
and the vats and bottles in the cavern, made a pleasant music
for the mind. Here, also, earth's cream was being skimmed
and garnered; and the London customers can taste,
such as it is, the tang of the earth in this green valley."

—Robert Louis Stevenson
The Silverado Squatters, 1880

There is an outfit in Burgundy that provides hot air balloon rides for visitors, and the ride presents entirely new perspectives on the great wine region. One can imagine such a ride on the North Fork of Long Island. Starting, perhaps, from a clearing in the middle of a Chardonnay vineyard in September, you step into the gondola of the balloon, surrounded by a seemingly endless sea of pampered vines, supporting clusters of pale green grapes. As the balloon rises, the winery and the house of the owner come into view, and you can see a mechanical harvester being readied for work. Soon there are neither clusters of grapes, nor individual vines, only perfect rows of lush green.

As the balloon rises higher the array of vines takes its place in a patchwork of potato fields, fruit trees and other vineyards. The villages seem incidental in the managed verdant landscape, punctuated by a surprising number of church spires. Narrow roads tie the scene together like ribbon around a parcel. Pickup trucks and cars inch along the roads. The yellow rectangle of a school bus moves even more slowly. The perspective is of a community which has spawned and nurtured its vineyards, and in which the wineries are playing an increasingly defining role.

Higher still, a new perspective appears. The scene is predominantly Atlantic blue. The narrow green strip of the North Fork, bounded by a thin border of tan beach, is defined by ocean waters. It seems fragile and vulnerable. To the west, the browns and black of roof tops and parking lots claim a larger share of the scene. Smog looms beyond Riverhead.

Style

Our imaginary balloon failed to float high enough to see California to the west or France to the east, but as the Island lies geographically, so Long Island wines lie stylistically between those two poles. Without the long dry sunny summers, Long Island wines will never have the strength or intensity of some of those from California. The milder maritime climate on the East End tends to produce grapes with somewhat less sugar, but it also can produce wines with more delicacy and refinement. Moreover, the sun shines more reliably and warmly on Cutchogue than it does on St Emilion, or on Gevrey Chambertin, for that matter. Long Island yields nothing to most of the vineyards of France in terms of the ripeness and intensity of its grapes.

An often heard refrain from the winemakers in the region is that fine wines are made in the vineyard. The quality of the grapes that can be grown here attracted many of them to Long Island. Tremendous care is devoted to the vineyards, and a common objective among the region's winemakers is to have their wines express the quality of the fruit that their vineyards produce. This is one reason why a majority of the wines on Long Island, and almost all of the best ones, are varietals, made predominantly from a single type of grape. Thus, a common stylistic element of many Long Island wines is their clear reflection of ripe varietal character.

Quality

There is no satisfactory way of comparing the quality of Long Island's wines to those of the rest of the world. If such questions had simple answers wine would be far less fascinating. Neither the subjects nor the objects of such comparisons are easily defined. There are mediocre wines produced in Bordeaux, for example, as well as superb ones. It is a naive and idle task to compare anything with the great wines of Burgundy or Germany. One should simply be thankful for them.

One can say, nonetheless, that despite its youth, Long Island has already produced wines of world class stature. Some selected Merlots, for example, have shown both a distinct style and a quality that can stand up to anything produced in this country. Chardonnays are arguably the region's most successful wines to date, and some have already rivaled all but the best available worldwide. The youthfulness of the region is underlined by the encouraging fact that from year to year one cannot predict which vineyard will produce the exceptional wine. There are other kinds of surprises. For example, recent tastings of wines from the vintages of 1980, 1983 and 1985 suggest that Long Island wines have much more potential for development in the bottle than previously thought.

For some time Long Island has been considered a promising wine region, and that remains its best characterization. The breadth and quality of the wines produced over the last few years have both confirmed that promise and raised the stakes. To achieve that ever higher promise, the identification of the region's most favored grape varieties needs further refinement. For reasons of winemakers' preferences, terroir and dictates of the market, certain grape varieties have become prominent on Long Island. The region seems to be able to produce competent wines from a wide range of grapes, however, and experimentation is far from over. Sparkling wines, for example, are receiving increasing attention, and advocates of Sauvignon Blanc, Cabernet Franc and other grape types are becoming more vocal. Over the next decade or two, one can expect that experimentation will lead to further focusing on those varieties and styles for which the Long Island terroir is found to be particularly well suited.

It is the coexistence of the vibrant, competitive aspirations of the winemakers and vineyard owners with the deeper, patient harmony of nature that defines one of the salient characteristics of Long Island wine country. The region has something of the entrepreneurial dynamism of Silicon Valley in the 1970s and something of the peacefulness of Kansas farmlands. This combination of intensity and harmony, of vibrancy and depth happens also to characterize great wines around the world. It is a high aspiration of the winemaker's art, and one that is more and more often being achieved on the East End of Long Island.

Reputation

In evolution there are environmental niches into which species fit. The population of the species must be a certain size to survive: too big and it exhausts its food supply; too small and it can not compete. Analogously, size and concentration have been important factors in the success of Long Island's growth as a wine region. In retrospect, there seems to have been about the right number of wineries for the region to grow efficiently. Had there been fewer, or had they been more widely scattered, there would not have been the critical mass from either a practical or intellectual point of view. The sharing of expensive equipment such as mechanical harvesters and bottling lines would not have been possible, and the international symposia that played an important educational and stimulative role may never have been organized. Further, the pioneering sense of a common fate and common interests that has stimulated the productive interactions between winemakers would have been missing.

Much more land on the East End of Long Island could be planted in vineyards. Some have estimated that the vineyard area could be expanded to as much as ten times the 1,600 acres or so now in grapes. Whereas some years ago, the vineyards sold a significant fraction of their production to wineries outside the region, local wineries now use virtually all of the grapes grown on the East End.

In the early days, Long Island wines were somewhat inconsistent, to the detriment of the region's reputation. More recently, the quality of the wines exceeds their reputation, in large part because the modest level of production does not allow, or justify, national distribution. Expansion of production would increase national and international reputation, with a concomitant increase in demand for these wines. A recent string of successful vintages, from 1990 to 1992, can only serve to enhance that reputation.

A major expansion of vineyards and wineries would only be good for the area if the new wineries exhibit the same obsession with quality that characterizes the best of the current establishments. That probably means a number of relatively small scale operations. Although the economic downturn of the early 1990s, together with the lessening of tax incentives, has had a dampening effect on new vineyard investments, this could well change in the near future. In fact, in late 1992, Sagapond Vineyards in Bridgehampton announced that its new winery would open in late 1993.

Romance

There is an apparent orderliness about winemaking: the strictly straight rows of vines combing the landscape; the precisely spaced vines along the trellis; oak barrels, with their own subtle geometry, carefully arrayed in a clean cellar; the perfect lattice of wine bottles in bins; and the solid geometry of stacked cases ready to be shipped. There is also the comforting mathematics of measurement: degree-days, yields and sugar content, Brix and pH. Financial projections of sales and profits are presented by quarter in the rows and columns of a spread sheet. Nature's precise regularity also adds to the seeming order: clock-measured days, calendar-measured months, and the sinusoidal variation of the seasons.

But the order is deceptive, cunningly designed to lure the unsuspecting into the life of a vineyard owner or winemaker. In the real world of winemaking, the regularities pale like the rectangular grid on old graph paper before the jagged lines that trace the irregular progress of grapes and wine. The last spring frost comes two precious weeks later than usual. A week of rain brings mildew that bursts the grape skins. Just as the grapes are achieving the right balance of carefully measured sugar and acid, flocks of thousands of starlings sweep down on the vineyard, ruin the careful work of a summer and peck away the future's profits. A hurricane roars through at harvest time.

Many prospective vineyard owners understand these hazards. After a few years in the business (or a few months) they certainly understand them. Still, they stay on. Why? If

Pindar winery seen from Lenz Vineyards.

you ask the winemakers of Long Island, the most commonly used word in their answer is "romance," a curious, old-fashioned word for a tough commercial activity.

The romance of winemaking is referred to sardonically as often as not—when the birds attack, or when pruning vines in the bone-chilling winds of February. But it is also said with a more profound meaning, referring to those experiences that are strongly felt, but difficult to articulate. Making wine is an activity that has some of the ineffable characteristics of a deep human relationship.

Sensitive visitors to the East End can get a lovely whiff of that romance. It hits you, like Cupid's arrow, when you are unsuspecting. You may fall under its spell one evening with a special friend, on the deck of a local restaurant overlooking the Sound, drinking an elegant wine made at a vineyard you have driven through that afternoon. Or it may happen on a late fall afternoon, when the captivating aroma of grapes fermenting in oak fills a vineyard's cellar. It can happen at any time, for romance is seldom rational.

Marco Polo, in his *Travels*, describes the elaborate repasts of an Oriental potentate: "When drink is called for, all who are present kneel down. At the same moment all the musical instruments, of which there is a numerous band, begin to play, and continue to do so until he has ceased drinking." Even without an actual band present, there is always a kind of music to a wine. Each wine has its own timbre and melody. Robert Louis Stevenson's "pleasant music for the mind" can be heard most clearly if one has visited the wine region and met the people who have made the wine. We urge you to do so.

Long Island Wine Country

MANHATTAN

QUEENS

BROOKLYN

STATEN ISLAND

NASSAU

(16)

SUFFOLK

ORIENT HARBOR

OR

GREENPORT

SHELTER ISLAND HEIGH

SOUTHOLD

PECONIC

(13)

(6)

(12)

(11)

(5)

(10)

(9)

CUTCHOGUE

NOYACK BAY

LITTLE PECONIC BAY

(48)

(7)

(8)

MATTITUCK

(4)

ROBINS ISLAND

(1)

SOUND AVE.

LAUREL

JAMESPORT

GREAT PECONIC BAY

BRIDGEHAMPTON

(25)

(2)

(3)

WATERMILL

25

RIVERHEAD

(14)

L.I. EXPRESSWAY 495

24

SOUTHAMPTON

(27)

SUNRISE HIGHWAY

SHINNECOCK BAY

THE EAST END

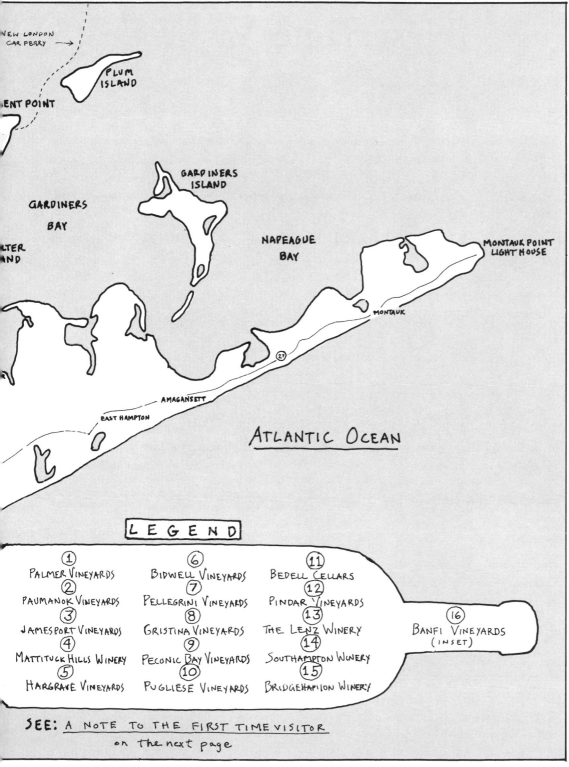

NEW LONDON CAR FERRY →

PLUM ISLAND

ENT POINT

GARDINERS ISLAND

GARDINERS BAY

LTER AND

NAPEAGUE BAY

MONTAUK POINT LIGHT HOUSE

MONTAUK

27

AMAGANSETT

EAST HAMPTON

ATLANTIC OCEAN

LEGEND

① PALMER VINEYARDS
② PAUMANOK VINEYARDS
③ JAMESPORT VINEYARDS
④ MATTITUCK HILLS WINERY
⑤ HARGRAVE VINEYARDS

⑥ BIDWELL VINEYARDS
⑦ PELLEGRINI VINEYARDS
⑧ GRISTINA VINEYARDS
⑨ PECONIC BAY VINEYARDS
⑩ PUGLIESE VINEYARDS

⑪ BEDELL CELLARS
⑫ PINDAR VINEYARDS
⑬ THE LENZ WINERY
⑭ SOUTHAMPTON WINERY
⑮ BRIDGEHAMPTON WINERY

⑯ BANFI VINEYARDS (INSET)

SEE: A NOTE TO THE FIRST TIME VISITOR on the next page

A Note to the
First Time Visitor

Planning a trip to Long Island wine country for the first time may appear daunting to the distant visitor, unfamiliar with the eastern end of the Island: How do we get there? What should we see? Where do we stay? Fortunately the wineries, except for Banfi, are clustered in an area of manageable size; one can drive the entire length of the North Fork from Riverhead to Orient Point at a leisurely pace in half an hour.

From New York City and points west the usual approach is the Long Island Expressway (Route 495) taken to Riverhead, the town that straddles the base of the two prongs of eastern Long Island, the North and South forks. From Riverhead, follow the signs to Greenport and Orient Point along Route 25. This takes one past nine wineries, one after the other, in the villages of Aquebogue, Jamesport, Mattituck, Cutchogue, and Southold.

From points north in New England there are two convenient ways of arriving: The ferry from Bridgeport to Port Jefferson, and the ferry from New London to Orient Point. From Orient Point there is an easy drive westward towards Riverhead. Entry at Port Jefferson requires that one follow Route 25A eastward, past a less-than-bucolic strip of suburban development, until the road splits at Wading River. Here one can proceed to the right towards Riverhead and Route 25, as above, or to the left along Sound Avenue. The second alternative is more scenic and leads past the other four wineries of the North Fork that are not on Route 25. Sound Avenue and its continuation, Route 48, parallel Route 25, and there are frequent connecting roads between the two. The wineries are all clearly indicated by signs, but we suggest that you check the visiting times shown in the boxed inserts at the end of each section in Chapter Four.

Visits to the wine country are most rewarding during the summer and early autumn months when the many farmstands offer a wealth of local fruits and vegetables, from berries and peaches to asparagus, squash and cauliflower. Ideally one should plan a country weekend that combines a visit to both the North and South Forks. Although there are a few restaurants that one can recommend on the North fork, including Ross's (see Chapter Five: Supporting Cast), one turns to the posher and slightly less rural South Fork for a wider array of dining experiences.

A lovely way to get to the south is by car ferry at Greenport toward Shelter Island, a ten minute trip, and then to follow signs to south ferry, a few miles down Route 114. From here there is another quick ferry trip to Sag Harbor, where one can drive to all points of the South Fork within twenty minutes or so, from East Hampton in the east to Bridgehampton in the middle. Westhampton Beach is a bit further west but is worth the detour to eat at Starr Boggs, the restaurant of the celebrated chef-owner of the same name, who has prepared the food for the annual Wine Spectator outdoor barbecue and barrel tasting hosted at a different winery on each occasion.

Sag Harbor and the Hamptons offer attractive inns for overnight lodging (book well in advance) as well as antique shops and spectacular ocean beaches, not to mention Bridgehampton Winery and Southampton Winery. Shelter Island itself boasts a few charming inns in an idyllic pastoral setting and is warmly recommended for an overnight stay because of its convenient location between the forks.

Bibliography

Aaron, Jan. *Wine Routes of America*. E. P. Dutton New York, 1989

Adams, Leon D.. *The Wines of America*. McGraw Hill, NY, 1990

Asher, Gerald. *On Wine*. Random House, NY 1982

Beltrami, Barbara and Edward Beltrami. "A Wine Weekend on Long Island," *Food and Wine*, May, 1992

————. "Wines of Eastern Long Island," *The Wine News*, June/July, 1991.

Blue, Anthony Dias. *American Wine: a Comprehensive Guide*. Harper & Row, N.Y., 1988

Clark, Corbet. *American Wines of the Northwest*. William Morrow and Company, 1989

Conaway, James. *Napa*. Houghton Mifflin Company, 1990

Cox, Jeff. *From Vines to Wines*. Garden Way Publishing, Story Communications, Inc., Pownal, VT, 1985

Darlington, David. *Angels' Visits: An Inquiry into the Mystery of Zinfandel*. Henry Holt and Co., New York, 1991

Digby, Joan and John, Eds.. *Inspired by Drink*. William Morrow and Company, NY, 1988

Goldenson, Suzanne. *Vintage Places: A Connoisseur's Guide to North American Wineries and Vineyards*. Main Street Press, Inc. Pittstown, NJ, 1985

Hargrave, Louisa. "A History of Wine Grapes on Long Island," *The Long Island Historical Journal*, Vol. 3 No. 1, p.3; Fall, 1990

Johnson, Hugh. *Vintage: The Story of Wine*. Simon and Schuster, New York, 1989

Kramer, Matt. *Making Sense of Wine*. William Morrow and Company, New York, 1989

Kramer, Matt. *Making Sense of Burgundy*. William Morrow and Company, New York. 1990

Laube, James. "Long Island Finds Its Style," *The Wine Spectator*, Nov. 30, 1988

Lawrence, R. de Treville, Ed.. *Jefferson and Wine*. Vinifera Wine Growers Association, The Plains VA, 1976

Lee, Hilde Gabriel and Allan E. Lee. *Virginia Wine Country*. Betterway Publications, White Hall, Va. 1987

Lynch, Kermit. *Adventures on the Wine Route*. Noonday Press, Farrar, Straus and Giroux, N.Y. 1988

Massee, William E.. *Joyous Anarchy: The Search for Great American Wines*. G. P. Putnam's Sons, N.Y. 1978

Matthew, Thomas. "Long Island's Summer Bash," *The Wine Spectator*, Sept. 30,1990

Matthews, Thomas. "Long Island Celebrates Home Grown Bounty," *The Wine Spectator*, Sept. 30, 1991

Meyer, Justin. *Plain Talk about Fine Wine*. Capra Press, Santa Barbara, California, 1989

Morton, Lucie T.. *Winegrowing in Eastern America*. Cornell University Press, Ithaca, NY, 1985

New York Senate Research Service, Task Force on Critical Problems for the Special Senate Majority Committee on the New York State Grape/Wine Industry. *Tending the Vineyards: Renewed Growth for New York's Grape/Wine Industry*. Albany, N.Y.,1984

Peynaud, Emile. *Knowing and Making Wine*. John Wiley, N.Y. 1984

Peynaud, Emile. *Le Vin et les Jours*. Dunod, Paris, 1988

Pinney, Thomas. *A History of Wine in America*. University of California Press, Berkeley, CA 1989

Robinson, Jancis. *Vines, Grapes and Wine*. Alfred A. Knopf, N.Y. 1986

Schoolsky, Robert, Ed. *Long Island Guide to Dining and Wining: 1990–1991*. Published by the Long Island Guide to Dining and Wining, 1990

de Vallee, Christine. "How the Vineyards Came to Long Island — A History: Long Island Wineries and the East End," *Times-Beacon Newspapers*, Setauket, N.Y. 1988

Winkler, A. J. et al.. *General Viticulture*. University of California Press, 1974

Zweig, Michael. "The Wine Industry and the Future of Agriculture on Long Island's North Fork," Research Paper No. 290, Department of Economics, State University of New York at Stony Brook, 1986

Index

acetic bacteria, 28
acidity, 26
Adams, Leon D., 2
Adlum, John, 32
Alexander, James, 32
Alsace , 14
Alsatian wine, 13
Anderson, R. Christian, 35-36
Australia, 8, 12

bacteria , 51, 80
Banfi Vineyards, 10, 21, 119-121
Barolo, 8
Barr, Alan, 44, 94 ff.
barrels (oak), 12, 29, 53, 110, 114
Bedell Cellars, 15, 44, 46, 72-77
Bedell, Kip, 22, 73 ff., 124
Bethel, Robert, 95
Bidwell Vineyards, 14, 15, 44, 80, 90-93
Bidwell, James, Kerry and Robert, 91
birds, 23
Blanc de Blanc, 12, 21, 120
Blanc Fumé, 13
blending, 29
Blum, Ray, 99, 109 ff.
Bordeaux Symposium, 41-42
Bordeaux, 1, 8, 16, 17, 51
botrytis, 13, 15, 22, 75
bottling tractor, 109
Brettanomyces, 68
Bridgehampton Winery, 14, 15, 40, 55-59, 80,
    99, 114, 124
budding, 16, 25
Bully Hill Winery, 56
Burgundian wines, 128
Burgundy, 3, 7, 8

Cabernet Franc, 16, 17 , 19, 135
Cabernet Sauvignon, 9, 10, 16, 17-18, 128
California 5, 8, 14
canopy management, 24
Carroll, Peter, 67 ff.

Castiglione Falleto, 8
Catawba, 32
Chablis, 13
Chambertin, 8
Champagne, 12, 18, 20, 21
Chardonnay, 10, 11-13, 69, 128, 134
Charmat, Eugene, 21
Château Lalande, 41
Château Le Bon Pasteur, 42
Château Margaux, 41, 46
Château Monbousquet, 43
Château Pétrus, 46
Chenin Blanc, 16
Chile, 12
climate, East End, 134
clones, 127
Coates, Clive, 25
Commonwealth Vineyards, 114
Concord (grape), 5
Cornell Agricultural Station, 99
Cornell Cooperative Extension Service, 123, 126
Cornell University, 37
Côte de Beaune, 12
coulure, 16
crop thinning, 26
crown gall, 127
cru , 7
crusher-stemmer, 27
Cutchogue 1, 2, 3, 34 , 36, 38
Cutchogue, 124

Damianos, Herodotus, 40, 57 ff.
Davids Farm, 73
de Lencquesaing, Mme., 41
degree days, 10
Denis, Donald, 85
dessert wine, 109
development rights, 11
Dijon, 3
Dom Pérignon, 31
Dorset Farms, 67
drainage, 22

East End, 34-39, 41
Environmental Protection Agency, 24

Farm Winery Bill, 39
Farmer Mike's, 129
Farmland Preservation Legislation, 39
fermentation, 27, 28, 51-52, 53
Finger Lakes, 33
Flatt, Charles, 109 ff.
Fournier, Moses "The Frenchman," 2, 34
Frank, Fred, 119
Frank, Konstantin, 2, 34, 37, 38, 119, 126
Franklin, Benjamin, 49
Friszolowski, Mark, 91 ff.
frost, 22, 26
Fry, Eric, 67 ff., 114, 119
Fumé Blanc, 13
fungi, 24

Gallo, 62
Gamay Beaujolais, 63
Genesis, 123
genetic engineering, 24
genetic structure, 31
Gevrey Chambertin 3
Gewürztraminer, 14, 34, 69
Gibbs, Colonel George, 33
glacier, 8
Goerler, Ronald Sr. and Jr., 103 ff.
Grape Advisory Committee, 128
grapes of Long Island, 10-20, 96
grapes, Barolo, 8; Catawba, 32; Cabernet Franc,
    16, 17 , 19, 135; Cabernet Sauvignon, 9, 10,
    16, 17-18, 128; Chardonnay, 10, 11-13, 69,
    128, 134; Concord, 5; Fumé Blanc, 13;
    Malbec, 18, 62; Merlot, 9, 16-17, 128, 134;
    Niagra, 10; per ton costs, 129; Pinot
    Meunier, 12, 18, 62, 64; Pinot Noir, 8, 12,
    17, 18-19, 22, 87, 103; Primitivo, 32;
    Riesling, 14-15, 34, 128; Sauvignon Blanc,
    13-14 , 128, 135; Seibel, 35; Semillon, 13;
    Seyval Blanc, 11, 126; Seyve-Villard, 35;
    Vitis riparia, 70; *Vitis labrusca,* 10; *Vitis
    vinifera,* 10, 70; Zinfandel, 32, 116
Grâves, 8
Greenfield, Lyle, 40, 41, 55 ff.
Gristina Vineyards, 18, 23, 24, 46, 83-89, 113

Gristina, Jerry and Carol, 84 ff.; Gristina, Jerry,
    113; Gristina, Peter, 84 ff.
groundwater supplies, 24

Hammondsport, 38
hand sorting, 26
Hanzell Vineyards, 12
Haraszthy, Count Agoston, 32
Hargrave Cabernet Sauvignon, 130
Hargrave Vineyard, 14, 15, 18, 21, 25, 49-54,
    130
Hargrave, Alex and Louisa, 1, 12, 13, 23 , 37-
    39, 80, 99; Hargrave, Alex, 41, 49 ff.;
    Hargrave, Louisa, 35, 49 ff.
harvest, 26
Hawaii, 63
Hearn, 96, 99, 113, 114
hedger, , 125
Henn, Bob, 63, 64
Hoffer, Bonnie, 129
Huguenot, 33
Hurricane Bob, 21, 24, 43
Hurricane Gloria, 43, 74
hurricane, 24, 25
hybrids, 10, 32, 33, 35, 36

irrigation, 125
Island Vineyards, 125
Iyres, Cynthia, 74
Iyres, Cynthia, 124

Jaffray, John, 92
Jamesport Vineyards, 14, 25, 103-105
Jefferson, Thomas, 17, 31, 32
Jefferson, Wayland, 35
John Tompkins, 38

Kleck, 50, 78 ff., 85, 90, 91
Klein, John, 40
Krupski, 129

lactic acid, 28
late harvest wine, 22
Le Rève Winery (Southampton Winery), 44,
    58, 94-97, 113
leaf plucker, 125
legislation, 39-40

Lenz Winery, 14, 18, 21, 46, 67-71, 80, 114, 119, 124

Lenz, Patricia and Peter, 14, 40, 67 ff.

Lobster Stew, 131 11

Long Island Sound, 9

Long Island Vintages, 43

Long Island Wine Council, 44, 45, 107, 124

Long Island Wine Growers' Association, 107

Loubat, Alphonse, 33

Lyme Disease, 44

Malbec, 18, 62

malic acid, 28, 68

malolactic fermentation, 12, 28

Marco Polo, 137

Mariani, John and Harry, 119

Massoud, Charles and Ursula, 98 ff.

Matt Kramer, 7

Matthews, Thomas, 95

Mattituck Hills Winery, 19, 106

McCullough, Sam, 69

mechanical harvester, 26, 84

Merlot Symposium, 42

Merlot, 9, 16-17, 128, 134

Meursault, 8, 12

Michelangelo, 1

Moët, 24

molds, 24

Mondavi Winery, 68

Mondavi, Robert, 13

Montrachet, 12

Morgan, Jeff, 23, 24

Morgan, Tom, 69

Morton, Lucie, 34

Mudd Vineyards, 124

Mudd, David, 40, 79, 85, 113, 123, 124, ff.

Muscat, 37

Napoleon, 3

New York Times, 2, 40, 46

New York Wine Experience, 46, 47

New Yorker, 2, 40

Niagra (grape), 10

Nissequogue, 33

North Fork Wine Services, 124-126

North Fork, 3, 9-10, 40, 134

Nugent, Phil, 46, 124

oidium, 33

Old Brookville, 21, 119

Olsen-Harbich, Richard, 14, 15, 19, 56 ff. , 84-85, 99, 114

"one-off" wines, 22

Oregon, 8, 47

Palmer Vineyards, x, 14, 15, 19, 41, 50, 74, 78, 125

Palmer, Robert, 19, 41, 78 ff.

Parmentier, André, 33

Pasteur, Louis, 28

Patzwald, Gary, 74, 80 ff.

Paumanok Vineyards, 15, 98-101

Peconic Bay Vineyards, 9, 80 , 99, 109-111

Pellegrini Vineyards, 96, 112-115

Pellegrini, Bob and Joyce, 112 ff.

Penn, William, 32

Pennsylvania, 33

Perrine, Larry, 84 ff.

pesticides, 24

Petit Verdot, 18, 62, 86

Peynaud, Emile, 50

phylloxera, 10, 24, 35

Pindar Vineyards, 14, 15, 18, 20, 21, 40, 61-65, 91, 130

Pinney, Thomas, 1

Pinot Blanc, 15, 51

Pinot Meunier, 12, 18, 62, 64

Pinot Noir, 8, 12, 17, 18-19, 22, 87, 103

Pontallier, Paul, 41, 42

Pouilly Fumé, 8

press wine, 28

Primitivo, 32

Prince, William, 32, 33

Prohibition, 34

pruning, 25

Pugliese Vineyards, 21, 116-117

Pugliese, Ralph and Patricia, 116-117

Quakers, 34

Querre, Alain, 43, 44

Rassepeage, 33

Ressler, Kirk and Richard, 123, 128 ff.

Ressler Vineyards, 74, 123, 128-129

restaurants, 3

Rheinfalz, 8
Riesling Trockenbeerenauslesen, 34
Riesling, 14-15, 34, 128
Riverhead, 3
Robinson, Jancis, 18, 19, 46
Rolland, Michel, 42
root stock, 24, 27
rosé wine, 19
Ross' North Fork Restaurant, 124, 129-131
Ross, John, 124, 129 ff.
Ruszits, 33

Sagapond Vineyards, 136
Santo Tomàs Vineyard, 62
Sauvignon Blanc, 13-14, 128, 135
Schoonmaker, Frank, 34
Seibel, 35
Semillon, 13
Sequin Moreau, 29
Seyval Blanc, 11, 126
Seyve-Villard, 35
Shanken, Marvin, 44
Simicich, John and Cathy, 106
Simicich, Richard, 106
Simon, Mark, 70
Simpson, Gretchen Dow, 55
Sisson, Ben, 128
site selection, 24
Smithtown, 33 3
soil, 8, 9, 68
Soundview Vineyards, 126
South Africa, 12, 16
South Fork, 9-10, 35
Southampton Winery, 94-96
Southampton, 35
Southold, 35
Southold, 124
sparkling wine, 19-20
Spooner, Alden, 35
spraying, 26
St. Emilion, 19
StevensonRobert Louis, 133, 137
Stony Brook Harbor, 33
sugar levels, 26
sulfur, 57, 68

tannin, 28, 86
tax laws, 125
Tchelistcheff, André, 62, 68
Tchelistcheff, Dimitri, 18 13, 62, 63, 92
terroir 1, 3, 4, 7-10
The Wine Spectator, 2, 44, 91, 95,
Thomas, Norman, 2, 50
Tompkins, John, 38
trellising, 13, 22, 24, 25, 127

University of California at Davis, 24, 57

Vanderbilt, Alfred, 119
vanillin, 29
varietals, 11, 51, 62, 126, 134
veraison, 26
vineyards, acres planted in, 125; expansion of, 136; siting of, 22
vinifera, 10, 126
vins de garde, 86
vins ordinaires, 64
Vitis labrusca, 10; *riparia,* 70; *vinifera,* 10, 70

Wagner, Philip, 34
Washington, George, 32
Waugh, Alec, 61
Wickham Fruit Farm, 1
Wickham, John, 35, 36-37, 38, 63, 126, 129
Wiemer, Hermann, 56, 57
Windows on the World, 124
wine consumption, 62
Wines of America, 2
winter damage, 17
Wisconsin glaciation, 8, 31
Wise, Alice, 123, 126

yeast, 9 28, 51, 68
yield, 27

Zellerbach, James, 12
Zinfandel, 32, 116

About the Authors & Photographer

Philip Palmedo, Sara Matthews, Edward Beltrami.

Philip Palmedo developed his interest in wines when he lived in Paris for two years in the mid-60s and visited all of the major wine regions. He has lived on Long Island for twenty-five years and was an early enthusiast of Long Island wines and the role that the industry could play in retaining the rural character of the East End of the Island. He received his BA degree from Williams and PhD from MIT, and has written widely on subjects ranging from energy and environmental policy to the relationship between art and science. He is President of the Long Island Research Institute and lives in St. James.

Over the years **Edward Beltrami** has written about wine for several leading publications, including *The Wine News, The Wine Spectator,* and *Wine & Spirits.* He lives in Setauket, Long Island, where he enjoys cooking with his wife Barbara, a food writer. A frequent and long time visitor to the viticultural regions of Europe, he is recognized as an expert on the wines of Italy, in addition to being a knowledgeable advocate for the wines of Long Island. Holding a doctorate in mathematics, he is on the faculty of the State University of New York at Stony Brook. He has published books on several areas of applied mathematics, the most recent of which is a Book of the Month selection for the *Library of Science.*

After earning a BS in architecture from Georgia Tech, **Sara Matthews** worked as an interior designer in New York before becoming a photographer specializing in what she loves: wine, food, people and travel. She lives in Brooklyn with her husband, Thomas Matthews, Senior editor for *The Wine Spectator,* and did the photographs for his upcoming book, *A Village in the Vineyards,* about their year in a small wine village near Bordeaux, France.

Also from **Waterline Books:**

Fish-Shape Paumanok

Nature and Man on Long Island

by Robert Cushman Murphy
Foreword by Steven C. Englebright

"A quiet classic of environmental wisdom,"
— Peter Matthiessen

"The Sand County Almanac of Long Island...Required reading...."
— Andrew Walker, Director
Long Island Chapter,
The Nature Conservancy

Available from your bookstore, or from
Waterline Books
438 River Bend Road
Great Falls, VA 22066

$9.95
83 pages
Illustrations by William Sidney Mount
Index
ISBN: 0-9628492-0-0

Please include $9.95 plus $1.50 for shipping when ordering from Waterline.